·COMPLETE·

Early Childhood BEHAVIOR MANAGEMENT *Guide*

COMPLETE

Early Childhood BEHAVIOR MANAGEMENT Guide

KATHLEEN PULLAN WATKINS ◇ LUCIUS DURANT, JR.

THE CENTER FOR APPLIED
RESEARCH IN EDUCATION
West Nyack, New York 10995

Library of Congress Cataloging-in-Publication Data

Watkins, Kathleen Pullan.
    Complete early childhood behavior management guide / Kathleen
Pullan Watkins, Lucius Durant, Jr.
      p. cm.
    Includes bibliographical references (p.) and index.
    ISBN 0-87628-261-3
    1. Early childhood education—United States. 2. Children—United
States—Conduct of life. 3. Behavior problems in children—United
States. 4. Classroom management—United States. I. Durant,
Lucius, 1932-   II. Title.
LB1139.25.W38 1992
372.11′024—dc20
                                        92-8261
                                        CIP

ISBN 0-87628-261-3

**The Center for Applied Research
in Education,** Professional Publishing
West Nyack, New York 10995
Simon & Schuster, A Paramount Communications Company

Printed in the United States of America

For Eric . . . because heroes are created
by encountering and conquering the
darkness . . .

For Gloria . . . my wife and my friend

ABOUT THE AUTHORS

Kathleen Pullan Watkins, Ed.D., is entering her twenty-second year as an early childhood educator/child development specialist. In addition to preschool/primary teaching experience, she has administered a number of programs serving young children and their families. Dr. Watkins has fifteen years' college teaching experience, during which time she has trained child care and social workers, and other human service professionals. She is currently a visiting lecturer in the Division of Behavioral Sciences at Community College of Philadelphia, an adjunct faculty member at Pennsylvania State University, and parent–child specialist at the Family Center of Thomas Jefferson University in Philadelphia. Dr. Watkins frequently consults for a wide range of businesses, and health and human service organizations in concert with her partner, Lucius Durant, Jr.

Lucius Durant, Jr., M.Ed., is an educator with thirty years' experience in classroom teaching, curriculum and program development, and administration. In recent years he has trained school personnel at every level. He is a frequent speaker and trainer on early childhood and general education topics. Mr. Durant is currently an adjunct professor at Community College of Philadelphia in the Early Childhood Education Program and at Pennsylvania State University in the Department of Individual and Family Studies. He has supervisory and oversight responsibility for the Division of Adult Education, School District of Philadelphia. Along with Dr. Watkins, Mr. Durant is the author of *The Preschool Director's Staff Development Handbook* and *The Complete Book of Forms for Managing the Early Childhood Program,* published by The Center, and *Day Care: A Sourcebook* (Garland Publishing).

ABOUT THIS RESOURCE

The *Complete Early Childhood Behavior Management Guide* provides you with the insight and tools you need to promote the best possible behavior in young children, as well as offering a storehouse of techniques for dealing with behavior problems when they occur. Any adult who works professionally with children from birth to age nine—whether in day care, preschool, primary school, youth associations, or other settings—will benefit from this handbook of practical information, guidelines, checklists, and ready-to-use forms.

The *Guide* shows you ways to head off problem behavior in young children by helping you understand their developmental needs and recognize factors in their environment that can precipitate problems. It shows you how to pinpoint inappropriate behavior, identify its causes, and work effectively with children and parents to overcome it.

In an approach both caring and practical, the GUIDE suggests positive ways to modify young chilren's behaviors through rewards and reinforcement, wisely applied punishments, and a number of alternative strategies. It recognizes both the teacher's need to maintain basic classroom control and the young child's need for self-expression in a safe, accepting environment.

Chapter One, "Why Discipline Can Be So Challenging," discusses ten common misconceptions about children's behavior, addresses parental stress and teacher self-esteem as factors in the problem, and concludes with the reasons problem behaviors must be addressed.

Chapter Two, "Developmental Influences on Early Childhood Behavior," offers a quick review of child development, with insights on how normal changes can effect child behavior and ways that caregivers can anticipate and either prevent or cope with normal episodes of difficult behavior.

Chapter Three, "Classroom Management for Better Behavior," shows how teachers and other adults affect classroom behavior, provides checklists for self-assessment, and suggests activities to help individual teachers and the entire staff work toward better child behavior.

Chapter Four, "Designing the Environment to Promote Good Behavior," provides checklists, evaluation worksheets, and specific techniques for creating classroom layouts, procedures, materials, rules, and routines that help children behave well.

Chapter Five, "Identifying Behavioral Problems," provides a variety of center-tested forms and techniques for getting to the root of any child's behavior problem.

Chapter Six, "Behavior Modification Techniques," gives numerous examples and suggests a wide variety of practical techniques for using punishment, rewards and reinforcement, and a variety of other strategies. It also lists common discipline errors and ways to avoid them.

Chapter Seven, "Referring Children for Special Services," describes when referrals are appropriate, discusses special education and abuse/neglect reporting, and provides forms and techniques for working with co-workers, parents, and outside agencies—including ways to build an effective referral network.

Finally, you will also find a handy list of resources for both parents and teachers.

The *Complete Early Childhood Behavior Management Guide* was written out of our long experience as early childhood professionals to help you with one of the most challenging tasks in working with young children—that of promoting the good behavior and classroom control you must have to provide a safe, happy environment for growth and learning. Working with young children can be very challenging and stressful. It is our sincere hope that this Guide will help you avoid some of that stress so that you can experience more of the joy of helping children grow.

Kathleen Pullan Watkins, Ed.D.

Lucius Durant, Jr., M.Ed.

CONTENTS

COMPLETE

Early Childhood

BEHAVIOR

MANAGEMENT

Guide

chapter one

WHY DISCIPLINE CAN BE SO CHALLENGING

As our society has become more complex and our social problems have grown and multiplied, so has our concern about child discipline and behavior problems. Psychologists and sociologists have made much of the link between childhood problems and difficulties that present themselves in later life. From talk-show guests to parenting guides the stress is on rearing a perfect, well-behaved child. Teachers of young children are increasingly being influenced by this emphasis.

The Shift in Child-Rearing Responsibility

In the first half of this century, child-rearing responsibilities were usually the jurisdiction of the family. When mothers were unable to care for children, grandmothers or other family members stepped in to assume this role. But by the late 1960s, increasing numbers of women were working outside the home. As we enter the last decade of this century more than half the mothers of preschool-aged children are employed, and this number is rising.

Sharing child-rearing responsibilities with the parents of the 1990s are thousands of teachers and child care workers. (The terms *teachers, child care workers,* and *caregivers* will be used interchangeably in this book.) These adults, some prepared for their roles and others untrained, have become surrogate parents and are faced with the same concerns and problems that the children's families face. Caregivers of young children are often pressured by parents to carry out the parents' wishes regarding the handling of problem behaviors. Many programs have no discipline policies that teachers can fall back on, so some of them must rely on their own child-rearing or family experiences as a basis for dealing with childrens' inappropriate behaviors.

Societal Changes That May Affect Child Behavior

Many of the societal issues focused on by the news media today stem from problems that may originate in childhood. Children who, for example, grow up in homes where addiction or abuse is present may repeat these behaviors in adulthood. Children of adolescent mothers are more prone to become parents themselves during the teenage years. In addition to these difficulties, American children are increasingly faced with problems of homelessness, divorce or other marital discord, and poverty.

Between initial exposure to a home problem and an unhappy outcome for an adolescent or young adult there may be many years of difficulty and unhappiness for a child. While still in infancy, the child may begin to feel the symptoms of this unhappy home life: rejection, anger, hostility. Adults who work with this child must be able to read and respond to these signals in an appropriate and effective fashion.

Perhaps since the very beginning of family life children have been seen as a reflection of their upbringing. Today more than ever, parents express concern that their children exhibit appropriate behaviors and experience successes at an early age. Middle-class children as young as two may have schedules as hectic as those of busy executives, with school, playgroups, and classes to attend. This pressure to prepare for adulthood while barely out of diapers has a stressful and ultimately negative impact on the developing child. Although some children are quite adaptable and manage to cope with adult expectations, others do not fare so well. They become tired and overwrought. They develop expectations for themselves not in keeping with their actual abilities and are angered and frustrated when they cannot perform as they would like to. Not permitted to be children, these youngsters are likely candidates for behavioral problems. Parents often need help to recognize that children may become stressed, just as adults do, by too many pressures. They may fail to recognize that childhood has specifically assigned developmental tasks. If this time is consumed by other activities, the child may fail to develop skills necessary for a healthy childhood and adult life.

While one caregiver cannot always be effective in changing a child's entire life, an adult who cares and understands can provide opportunities for the growth of new behaviors—new ways for a child to respond to stresses and challenges.

Developmental Changes and Child Behavior

Not all behavioral problems can be traced to family situations. Many aspects of normal development are confusing to adults and can appear to be problems. Children can change dramatically from one growth phase to the next. Along with the physical changes that are evident come cognitive and psychosocial developments that can cause a child to be difficult, argumentative, uncooperative. Adults involved with that child may need to reconsider the techniques previously used for interaction. In fact, most children go through fairly stressful and significant changes each time they enter a new period of growth.

Although most adults consider themselves well versed in child development and needs—after all, weren't we all once children ourselves—in fact, many are unfamiliar with the behaviors produced by developmental changes. Well-intentioned grown-ups may misinterpret the ordinary symptoms of growth and attribute to the child the thinking and manipulative behaviors of adults. Teachers and parents alike may believe that early behavioral or discipline problems may signal more serious difficulties in the future. It is important that every child's potential for growth and change be recognized and that adults avoid labeling children who fail to meet their expectations.

Here are two examples of how children's behavior can be misinterpreted by adults unfamiliar with aspects of development.

> A little girl made a trip to visit her grandparents, who were living in another state. At age three this little girl's language was well developed, and her conversational skills were exceptional. However, since seeing her grandparents last she had added some new phrases to her repertoire. Thus, when someone would say, "Courtney, you look nice!" Courtney would respond, "You've got that right!" On hearing this, a family friend chuckled and said, "What a fresh little girl!"

But was Courtney really being "fresh"? The answer is *no!* Courtney was experiencing a period of rapid language growth. During this time she extracted not just new words but entire phrases from every available source—adult conversations, television shows and commercials, even stories read to her by her parents. Therefore, a three-year-old like Courtney successfully mimics what adults say, even managing to say things at seemingly "appropriate" times without really understanding what she is saying. Spurred by the reactions of the adults (who may appear surprised or shocked, or chuckle), Courtney is more likely to repeat the offending phrase.

This next scene was recently witnessed in a Head Start center:

> Unaware that she was being observed by a program consultant, a parent emerged from the center reception area with her four-year-old son. As the door closed behind them the child called good-bye to the staff. The parent yanked the little boy by the arm and said, "What do you mean 'Good-bye' (mimicking the young child's voice). Can't you put some bass in this voice?"

This parent was clearly disturbed by some idea that her young son's high-pitched voice was a symptom of some feminine tendencies. To many parents, afraid of AIDS, pedophilia, and homosexuality, even the normal pitch of a young child's voice can seem threatening. It was apparently seen by this parent as a sign of some problem to come that might be nipped in the bud by maternal input. Unfortunately, this parent may do harm to her child's identity by interacting with him in this way. Teachers need to discuss this problem with the parent and provide support and a referral, if necessary, for counseling.

A form called "Check Your Parenting Stress Level" is provided here as a tool for early childhood professionals interested in helping parents see how their own emotions and behaviors affect those of their children. Teachers may want to check the levels of their own stress, as it can influence how they interact with children in the classroom. Consider the use of this checklist during a parents' meeting when the topic of discipline is being discussed.

Are There Really More Discipline Problems Today?

When the authors of this book first worked with preschool and primary grade children, serious problems were a rarity. Teachers were able to focus primarily on the scope of normal development and on programming issues. The role of teachers in the 1990s, however, has greatly expanded. Today children coming to school bring with them many more stresses and problems, and consequently more discipline problems. The scope of a teacher's knowledge must be greater today, along with his preparation to respond to a wide range of children's problems. Few teachers, however, have adequate preparation. As a result, the range of teacher concerns is vast, but chief among these is the issue of discipline. Every aspiring teacher envisions a tightly run classroom where children are appropriately respectful and obedient; envision the handicapping effects that a single disruptive child can have on a class's functioning.

What preparation teachers do receive now may be ineffective because many have trouble integrating what they have learned into actual practice. They may agree in principle with what they have been taught about development, but when confronted with the behaviors of real children, they often simply adhere to the rules set down by their own parents. After all, these are the most familiar methods. When our parents were growing up, certain ideas about child rearing were accepted by virtually everyone, although in many cases this was partly based on religious beliefs, partly on superstition, and partly on "old wive's tales." Many of

Check Your Parenting Stress Level

Directions: Parents are often overwhelmed by home and child-rearing responsibilities. Sometimes those stresses influence the behavior of their children—the child picks up on and reacts to parents' concerns. This checklist is one way you can tell whether stress is complicating your parenting responsibilities. Mark each statement *true* or *false,* according to your perspective.

_____ 1. I am a single parent.

_____ 2. I am a working parent.

_____ 3. I have more than one child.

_____ 4. I have more than one child under the age of five.

_____ 5. I attend school (high school, college, training) part time or full time.

_____ 6. I sometimes care for one or more extended family members.

_____ 7. I have little time for recreation or fun.

_____ 8. My income is often insufficient to meet my needs.

_____ 9. I would like to move to a new neighborhood.

_____ 10. I have no family members living nearby.

_____ 11. My child behaves poorly a lot of the time.

_____ 12. I often have to do things for my child to avoid a mess.

_____ 13. My child asks too many questions.

_____ 14. My child has a lot more energy than I do.

_____ 15. My child watches television more than I would like.

_____ 16. My child often has temper tantrums.

_____ 17. I have to spank my child frequently.

_____ 18. I often have to raise my voice to get my child to listen.

_____ 19. There has recently been a death in my family.

_____ 20. I have gone through a recent separation or divorce.

_____ 21. I have recently been ill.

_____ 22. I am frequently depressed or anxious.

_____ 23. My spouse and I are both working parents.

_____ 24. I have recently moved.

_____ 25. I am often fatigued or tired.

these ideas have persisted into the 1990s, and competent teachers of young children must face them head on and refuse to allow them to influence their interactions with children.

Filling out "Check Your Discipline Attitudes," provided here, is one way you can examine your own values and attitudes. We recommend that you fill it in before you read the following discussion of some popular misconceptions about child rearing. This material also works well at a meeting where staff can share thoughts about the origins of their values and ways of overcoming inappropriate attitudes.

Ten Common Misconceptions About Child Behavior

1. *The bad seed:* A child who demonstrates serious misbehavior during the preschool years is probably unsalvageable. This is based on a belief that children inherit badness or evil ways from their parents, just as they might inherit eye or hair color.

   The early childhood principle: While some aspects of personality may be inherited (researchers are still studying this), children are not born "bad." They may be born into poor environments that fail to stimulate and nourish them. They may have few or poor role models on which to base appropriate behavior. They do not, however, inherit genes for evil. All children have opportunities to be influenced by positive aspects of their environment, provided they have not been unfairly labeled by adults. For children to reach their potential some caring adult must recognize and stimulate the growth of that potential. These positive experiences must overtake and overwhelm negative ones in either quantity or quality.

2. *Spare the rod:* Some children do not respond to any reprimands other than spanking. There is an old biblical adage that suggests that failure to punish, and punish harshly, results in a spoiled, undisciplined child.

   The early childhood principle: Research clearly shows that harsh punishment causes negative psychosocial reactions in children. While some children withdraw, others may become openly hostile and resentful. In both cases they suffer a loss of self-esteem. Punishment is necessary and effective in many cases, but it must be suited to the child's age or development and to the misbehavior. Punishment must never be doled out in anger, but meted out thoughtfully. Corporal punishment of children (spanking or slapping) is never advisable.

Check Your Discipline Attitudes

Evaluating your own perspectives and attitudes about discipline is one step in developing effective behavior management skills.

Directions: Mark each statement either *true* or *false* depending on your perspective. A discussion of each statement follows in the next section.

_____ 1. A child who demonstrates serious misbehavior during the preschool years is probably unsalvageable.

_____ 2. Some children do not respond to any reprimands other than spanking.

_____ 3. Shaming a child in front of peers is a good way to encourage cooperation with adults.

_____ 4. The old "tried-and-true" methods of discipline used by our grandparents are the most effective.

_____ 5. Young children who lie will probably develop into chronic liars in adulthood.

_____ 6. When a young child appears guilty it means he has probably done something wrong.

_____ 7. Children's misbehavior is a clear-cut sign of poor parenting.

_____ 8. It is acceptable for boys to be more rough and aggressive in their play than girls.

_____ 9. Girls should exhibit more "ladylike" and gentle behaviors in their play than boys.

_____ 10. Classroom problems are usually started by the same children.

3. *Shame on you:* Shaming a child in front of peers is a good way to encourage cooperation with adults.

   The early childhood principle: Very early in development, by the end of the second year, children develop a degree of self-awareness. Along with this comes the capacity to experience embarrassment and shame. When children are embarrassed by their own behavior or an accident, they feel uncomfortable, but the sensation is generally short-lived. Shame that is deliberately provoked by an adult is, however, another issue. The loss of self-esteem and confidence experienced under these circumstances can create long-term problems for children. Furthermore, they may adopt shaming techniques as a way of interacting with others.

4. *If it was good enough for me:* The old "tried-and-true" methods of discipline used by our grandparents are the most effective. Quite naturally, many adults feel that their parents did an adequate job of rearing them. They forget their parents' errors and extol their virtues. It is, therefore, difficult for many adults to understand why older methods of child rearing and discipline are now being called inappropriate.

   The early childhood principle: Of course, many parents in the past did an excellent job rearing their children without benefit of child care handbooks or experts in the field. There were, however, many hidden problems in families, including child abuse and neglect. Research shows that some children handle even severe stress well. They are resilient and bounce back from the impact of family problems and parenting disorders. Some children do not bounce back so easily, however. They are seriously scarred by the problems they encountered in early childhood. Many benefits can be derived from our current knowledge of child development and child care practices. These include guidelines that facilitate the most positive adult–child interactions. Since we do not know which children might be harmed by stresses and which ones are resilient, it is best always to utilize those child-rearing techniques that are less risky to the child.

5. *Liar, liar, pants on fire:* Young children who lie will probably develop into chronic liars in adulthood. To adults, lying is an indication of personality flaws. Liars are bad people.

   The early childhood principle: Throughout most of early childhood children have no notions of the difference between truth and lies. Characteristics of thinking during this developmental phase include confusion between fantasy and reality. Children between the ages of two and eight years may believe in talking animals and flowers. They may believe that storybook and movie ghosts, monsters, and witches will come to spirit them away during the night. These children may see a cartoon or movie and incorporate it into an event they are recounting. After watching the movie *The Black Stallion* a little boy told a fantastic yarn about a trip to Africa he had taken with his parents and all the animals he had seen. Was he lying? Not at all. He was using language and imagination creatively. Some children will also invent stories to protect themselves from adult disapproval and punishment. Young children base their moral decisions on these criteria rather than on any concepts of right and wrong.

6. *Guilty as charged:* When a young child appears guilty it means he has probably done something wrong. Many people feel that certain behaviors like downcast eyes, foot shuffling, and mumbling are indications of guilt. They believe that a child who hides items, who closes his bedroom door, or who abruptly stops an activity when adults enter the room is probably doing something he should not be doing.

   The early childhood principle: When children are suspected of wrongdoing they often appear guilty, whether they are or not. If adults approach them frequently with the questions, "What are you up to now? What have you been getting into?" children will develop concerns and fears that they are going to get into trouble, and this worry shows in an embarrassed stance and difficulty in making eye contact. It is also true, however, that children sometimes live up to our expectations, be they positive or negative. A child who is always suspected of wrongdoing may get into trouble more frequently to assure adult attention.

7. *The fruit doesn't fall far from the tree:* Children's misbehavior is a clear-cut sign of poor parenting. Very often adults who observe the acting-out behavior of young children shake their heads sadly and reflect on the poor parenting evidently occurring in that child's family. Children have always been seen as a direct reflection of parental input; when they are quiet and well behaved their parents are praised, but when they are ill tempered or rude, society views their parents with stony disapproval.

   The early childhood principle: Even from the day of birth children have unique personalities. Although they do inherit certain characteristics from their parents, the mixture of traits in each person is unique. Thus, while inheritance is truly an important factor in development, as is the input that children receive from their environment, there is no established or predictable rate regarding the strength of either of these influences. In some cases parental input weighs heavily in developmental outcomes. In other situations secondary factors may be more influential.

8. *Boys will be boys:* It is acceptable for boys to be more rough and aggressive in their play than girls. Many adults believe that being male means coming into this life with more than your share of hormones for competitiveness and aggression. Adults have come to accept and expect that boys will demonstrate more acting-out behavior, get into more fights, and demand more attention.

   The early childhood principle: Many aggressive behaviors are learned by both boys and girls from the environments in which they grow up. When children are urged to develop in well-rounded ways that emphasize all of their positive traits, a balance of characteristics that is neither distinctly male nor female often results. As they are growing up, children of both sexes should be helped to develop both assertiveness (so they can state and protect their needs) and nurturing qualities (needed in intimate relationships throughout life).

9. *Sugar and spice and everything nice:* Girls should exhibit more "ladylike" and gentle behaviors in their play than boys. Girls are often believed to be by nature less assertive and less capable of meeting their needs than boys. Parents and teachers prefer and nurture traits of submissiveness, gentility, and soft-spokenness in female children. Terms like *tomboy* are applied to girls who do not demonstrate appropriately feminine characteristics.

   The early childhood principle: Girls are as capable as boys of self-sufficiency but only when provided with opportunities and encouragement to acquire the requisite skills. Urging girls to be clear about their needs, to defend their property, and to take leadership roles in play is difficult for some adults, who themselves were reared in a different social climate. However, failure to facilitate children's growth toward reaching their full potential is akin to deliberately handicapping them.

10. *The troublemaker:* Classroom problems are usually started by the same children. Many adults believe that if a child is prone to causing problems or disruptions in early childhood this can develop into a life-long trait. When a group of children play together and trouble erupts they believe this same child is usually the cause of the difficulty.

    The early childhood principle: A number of issues are involved in exploring this misconception. One is that adults interfere far too often in children's problems. Left alone, children will resolve many of their own difficulties. Children have ways of letting other children know when their behavior is undesirable. They will often ostracize a bully or showoff. Second, many very energetic, outgoing, and hard-to-handle preschoolers turn into perfectly reasonable school-aged children. With maturity they are able to channel their energies more effectively and learn the social skills needed for coping with other children.

Discipline and Effective Teaching

Although it would be wrong to generalize about all teacher training and education programs, there are some criticisms that it is reasonable to make. Precious few of the colleges and universities that prepare adults to work with young children spend adequate time teaching students about child development and behavior. Instead, they focus on the content areas. We learn about teaching children to read, teaching them math and science concepts, and teaching them social studies. Indeed, teachers and care-givers need this information. They would not be able to create or implement curriculum without it.

Unfortunately, however, it is not until student teaching and practicum experiences are over and we are ensconced in our classrooms that we realize the awful truth. If we cannot capture and hold children's attention, if we cannot stop disruptive behavior, we seldom get a chance to do any meaningful teaching. It is our heartfelt belief that herein lies the reason that so many teachers are victims of job burnout. As idealistic young teachers, first starting out in the profession, they envision their classrooms as tightly run ships. The children are busy, happy, and productive. The teachers are knowledgeable and supportive. Children's gains are measured not in inches but by leaps and bounds. These teachers dream of making a real difference in children's lives. But what really happens is a stark and discouraging contrast to the dream. Without innate skills or adequate training most teachers face a chaotic environment in which children demand attention, quarrel and cry, and sometimes hit one another. They call each other names, and their family problems come to school with them.

Teachers soon become discouraged and may spend the largest portion of their time disciplining. All their plans for a happy, busy classroom, where children are helped to reach their potential, go up in smoke. Without resources for coping with these problems many teachers give up. They stop teaching and focus on keeping children under control. Or, if they fail to do this, they are subject to criticism from supervisors and parents.

The checklist "How Effective Is Your Teaching?" provided here, is designed to help teachers look at the relationship between classroom management and effective program implementation. It is a way for the

How Effective Is Your Teaching?

Directions: Use this checklist to determine whether discipline problems are interfering with the operation of your classroom. If you are able to answer *yes* to three or more of the items below, classroom management may be a problem in your classroom.

	Yes	No
1. My classroom is often loud and noisy.	_____	_____
2. I have more than two children in my classroom who have frequent behavior problems.	_____	_____
3. I must speak to at least two parents per week about their children's behavior in school.	_____	_____
4. I find myself frequently saying "no," "don't," and "stop" to the children in my classroom.	_____	_____
5. I often have to alter or abandon my lesson plans because the children are uncooperative.	_____	_____
6. Special activities in my classroom are often disrupted by the same children.	_____	_____
7. I think of the children in my classroom as being largely uncooperative.	_____	_____
8. My co-worker and I disagree about the handling of the children in our classroom.	_____	_____
9. I do not get support for handling children's problems from my supervisor.	_____	_____
10. I do not get support for handling children's problems from their parents.	_____	_____

teaching staff to determine how much energy goes into controlling the group versus providing a good learning environment for children. Used at a staff meeting or in-service training session, this checklist can help stimulate discussion about what is really important for young children.

How Teacher Self-Esteem Affects Classroom Management

How teachers and caregivers feel about themselves as professionals is strongly influenced by their success in the classroom. But this concept also works in the reverse; that is, the self-esteem that teachers bring to the classroom affects their success there.

For example, to get others to comply with our wishes we must display authority and self-confidence. Even young children will respond better to a confident child than they will to one lacking in self-esteem. Adults with a gentle yet firm presence generally have more success with children than those who are hesitant or use anger to get children to comply.

Our self-esteem also influences our interactions with other adults. If we lack self-esteem we are more likely to have conflicts with co-workers and parents. Poor self-esteem colors our perceptions of others and how they feel about us. We may feel threatened or challenged when others try to help us or ask for our help. We may tend to be less giving if poor self-esteem forces us to guard our skills and knowledge jealously out of an unwarranted fear that others will use what we know to hurt us.

Conflicts among adults offer little in the way of behavior modeling for the children they care for. While children may not understand all of the reasons why adults interact as they do, children can observe for themselves how adults interact together. Tension among caregivers can be interpreted by children as a cause for anxiety and concern—and higher stress in children can lead to many forms of acting-out behavior.

By contrast, a high level of self-esteem has many benefits in the classroom. The inevitable problems with children and with other adults are not taken as personally. Teachers with good self-esteem are less territorial, so they are less likely to feel threatened by other adults or by children's behavior. Adults who are confident about their skills are more likely to share and demonstrate cooperative behaviors themselves.

It is very difficult to facilitate children's self-esteem if your own is poor. If teachers feel positively about themselves they focus on the needs of the children rather than on their needs. Try using the checklist "Rate Your Professional Self-Esteem," provided here, to determine whether poor self-esteem affects your classroom management and the children's behavior.

Rate Your Professional Self-Esteem

Directions: Read the statements below and rate each statement on a scale from one to five, with five meaning that you strongly agree and one meaning that you disagree. After rating each statement total the number of points you have received. Forty points or more indicates a high level of self-esteem; thirty or more points suggests that your self-esteem is adequate; and less than thirty points indicates that you should work on raising your professional self-esteem.

_____ 1. My co-worker and I share many new ideas for the classroom.

_____ 2. My co-worker's ideas are usually very good.

_____ 3. My co-worker likes and uses my ideas.

_____ 4. My activities for my classroom are usually successful.

_____ 5. The children enjoy working with me.

_____ 6. The children are usually responsive to my commands and directions.

_____ 7. Parents of children in my classroom like me.

_____ 8. I am usually able to work out problems with parents successfully.

_____ 9. I am anxious to learn more about teaching and to improve my skills.

_____ 10. I rarely yell at the children or scold them.

© 1992 by The Center for Applied Research in Education

The Need to Address Children's Behavior Problems

In this chapter we have examined adult attitudes toward discipline and behavior problems and have addressed the fact that many behavior problems may originate in adult feelings and concerns. But many behavior problems are real, and when they do occur they can seriously disrupt children's opportunities for learning and development.

A child who is disruptive in the classroom is distracted from learning. She is unable to take advantage of events, materials, and interactions that teach. Her learning potential is further interrupted by the way adults are often involved with her. Instead of having positive interactions with her teachers, this child is often scolded or punished. Adults are less inclined to extend themselves to her to teach or to answer a question because they do not enjoy being with her. They may even resent the time they have to spend disciplining her, instead of teaching the other children.

Children with behavior problems also suffer socially. They are often outcasts. Other children may not want to play with them. They are left out of games and play. When included, their play may have unhappy outcomes. They may miss chances to develop physical skills, to learn concepts, and to develop survival skills, all of which are derived from play.

Some behavior problems of young children are a direct result of their developmental level. As they pass through each of the stages addressed by this book, children experience physical, cognitive, and psychosocial changes that have a marked impact on their behavior. Understanding these changes is taking one step toward decreasing any negative effects on children. In the next chapter we will explore these developmental influences as children progress through infancy, toddlerhood, the preschool years, and middle childhood.

chapter two

DEVELOPMENTAL INFLUENCES ON EARLY CHILDHOOD

Child development, especially in early childhood, is characterized by a series of changes that accompany each phase. These changes occur in the three primary areas of physical, cognitive, and psychosocial growth. Although there is constant change in each area, rarely is the rate of growth the same in every area. And although child development is sequential, the amount and pace of development varies greatly from one child to another. Interactive processes are at work; that is, the three aspects of development influence one another. Cognitive growth influences psychosocial development, physical development may affect cognitive growth, and so on.

In this chapter we will examine the variety of ways in which development, and the interactive processes inherent in it, influence child behavior. We will also suggest appropriate adult responses to the many behavioral changes occurring in early childhood.

Developmental Changes in Infancy

The quiz "Test Your Knowledge of Infant Behavior," provided here, will help you check your knowledge of what "normal" infant behavior is. Understanding what is developmentally normal helps adults who work with young children eliminate misconceptions about inappropriate behavior during this first phase of early childhood.

Most adults do not consider the nonmobile newborn to be a source of behavior problems. The baby, by virtue of her cry, odor, body movements, and other features, inspires in the average adult a strong desire to take care of her, to see to her physical and emotional needs. Infancy is, in fact, a kind of testing ground for the baby in the development of

Test Your Knowledge of Infant Behavior

Directions: Read each statement carefully and select the appropriate response from the choices offered.

1. Physical, cognitive, and psychosocial milestones occur

   a. simultaneously.

   b. without impacting on one another.

   c. at different rates while impacting on one another.

2. Grasping, crying, sucking, and rooting are examples of infant

   a. learned behaviors.

   b. reflexes.

   c. cognitive skills.

3. Colic is thought to be related to

   a. gas pains or indigestion.

   b. the central nervous system.

   c. infant temperament.

4. Sudden crying or dropping off to sleep may be a sign of _____ in an infant.

   a. overstimulation

   b. colic

   c. illness

5. When infants are born their senses are

   a. as acute as those of adults.

   b. working but not all as acutely as adult senses.

   c. nonfunctional.

Test Your Knowledge of Infant Behavior (continued)

6. Object permanence develops when an infant is able to

   a. mentally represent a person or object.

   b. realize his effect on the environment.

   c. manipulate the environment.

7. A strong attachment relationship with an adult is _____ to an infant's psychosocial functioning.

   a. not essential

   b. not relevant to

   c. critical to

8. Infants reaching for, clinging to, and smiling at caretakers is an indication of

   a. insecurity.

   b. secure attachment.

   c. emotional disturbance.

9. Fearful responses in infants to strange people, places, or things should be

   a. treated as normal.

   b. punished.

   c. discouraged.

10. Responding regularly to infant cries or needs

    a. leads to the development of basic trust in the infant.

    b. leads to spoiling.

    c. does not affect the child.

Answer Key: 1. c.; 2. b; 3. b; 4. a; 5. b; 6. a; 7. c; 8. b; 9. b; 10. a

skills for survival in the world. She must find her place in the immediate world to successfully navigate through life. The infant does this in many exciting and challenging ways.

Physical Growth and Infant Behavior

Newborns come equipped with a set of reflexive behaviors that signal their earliest responses and reactions to the world around them. Crying is a reflex, as are sucking, rooting, and grasping at objects. Infant crying is one of the concerns of many caregivers and parents. As a reflexive behavior, crying is not planned by the baby. It is triggered, much like a yawn or sneeze, by some stimulus, such as hunger pangs, cold, or a wet diaper. The young infant has few tools for comforting herself. The sucking reflex is one of these. She relies on adult caregivers to relieve the source of stress, which in turn stops the crying. Rocking an infant, feeding, and changing a soiled diaper are ways in which ordinary caregiving tasks comfort a baby and can stop crying behavior.

There are, however, other sources of distress less easily determined. Many young babies experience a period in which they are colicky. This is a catchall term for a series of symptoms that often lead to prolonged infant crying and restlessness. Although the caregiver exercises the normal responses to the baby's crying, the fretfulness continues.

Experts in development continue to be somewhat puzzled by colic, but recent research suggests that the central nervous system of some babies may need to emit a kind of discharge, perhaps as another tool for infant survival.

While infants enjoy play and interaction with adults and with their environment, they sometimes experience a type of sensory overload. The newborn's brain is still developing, so babies may become overwrought when environmental demands are too great for them to handle. A baby's happy cooing or babbling can suddenly disintegrate into inconsolable crying if she has been frightened or has had too great an input of noise, light, or activity. Some babies just drop off to sleep when they have had enough. In either case, they are temporarily shutting down their centers for sensory input.

A quiz for matching "Infant Behaviors and Appropriate Responses" is provided in the box. It can be used by those caring for infants as a basis for discussion about caregiving practices. A second box provides some tips for comforting crying or distressed infants.

One of the greatest challenges of early infancy is for the baby to develop initial control of her body. For example, the infant gradually gains control of her neck, back, and abdominal muscles, enabling her to lift her head, roll over, sit up, and crawl. These set the stage for walking

Infant Behaviors and Appropriate Responses

Match the five infant behaviors on the left with the appropriate response.

_____ 1. Infant coos or babbles.

_____ 2. Infant cries abruptly during play.

_____ 3. Infant clings to adult in presence of a fearful stimulus.

_____ 4. While in a high chair, infant purposely, repeatedly drops spoon.

_____ 5. Infant cries continuously without apparent reason.

a. Ignore the behavior.

b. Push the infant away.

c. Talk to the infant.

d. Remove the spoon.

e. Punish the infant.

f. Stop the game.

g. Remove the cause of the fear.

h. Continue the game.

i. Allow the behavior to continue.

j. Find the source of the problem; comfort as needed.

Answer Key: 1. c; 2. f; 3. g; 4. i; 5. j

© 1992 by The Center for Applied Research in Education

Comforting a Distressed Infant

Prolonged infant crying is stressful to both adult and baby. Sometimes it even appears contagious; when one baby cries the rest may join in. Here are a few "tried-and-true" techniques for use with infants under twelve months.

- Rock the infant in a rocking chair.

- Place the infant in a wind-up swing.

- Turn on a music box or soft musical selection.

- Place the baby on her stomach and rub her back using a small circular motion.

- Swaddle the baby in a blanket and rock her (works best with infants under six months).

- Lay the infant on her back and gently stroke her forehead, eyelids, and cheeks with your fingertips.

- Talk or sing softly to the baby while rocking her.

- Give the infant a bottle or pacifier (remove the bottle after the infant is asleep).

- Take the baby outdoors for a ride in the coach or car.

- Provide an interesting distraction such as keys, a colorful block, or plush toy; talk softly as you show the toy to the infant.

behavior in the second year. They are the real precursors to the exploration of the physical environment essential to cognitive development in childhood.

Cognitive Growth and Infant Behavior

Contrary to the assertions of seventeenth-century philosopher John Locke, infants are not "blank slates" at birth. Rather, they are born with functioning senses and with impressions received even while in the womb. Although some senses function poorly at first, like sight and taste, hearing and touch are acute. Even during the first weeks of life babies are soaking up information from the surrounding environment. The sounds of voices and other noises around them are all taken in. They carefully scan their surroundings, focusing their attention on what they can see most easily: usually objects twelve to fourteen inches from their faces. They are attracted to geometric patterns, human faces, and bright colors. They absorb sensations from their bedclothes and from the touches of their caretakers. During each of these experiences they are learning.

Piaget tells us that initially infants do not comprehend their influence on the environment. They see no relation between their own crying and the appearance of adults to comfort and care for them. Gradually, however, they recognize this connection. With this awareness comes the beginning of some manipulation of the environment to achieve favorable ends. Does this mean that infants are capable of manipulative behavior? Indeed not! Babies are merely trying out, experimenting, to see what activities will produce similar or different results. They do not know how to "play games," as adults like to put it, with the feelings and needs of others. Babies are egocentric. They think the world is centered around them, and they do not recognize the effects of their behavior on others. They are incapable of selfishness because they cannot yet choose between their own needs and those of others.

Another facet of cognitive growth in infancy is the development of object permanence. This refers to the child's understanding that objects and people continue to exist when no longer in sight. Connected to the growth of memory and the ability to mentally represent ideas, object permanence also signals psychosocial changes.

Psychosocial Development and Infant Behavior

The first and most significant of human relationships is that of parent to child. It is the forerunner of all significant relationships in the human life span. When the parent–child relationship is strong and positive, chances are good that the other human interactions that follow will be similarly rewarding for the child.

At birth infants do not distinguish one adult from another. However, within just a few months of birth they are capable of exhibiting unique behaviors toward those persons most involved with their daily care. They reach for, smile to, and permit themselves to be comforted by the adults they are most familiar with. This reaction does not always sit well with adults who cannot comprehend a baby's distressed reaction to unfamiliar faces and places.

Fearful responses to strangers typically manifest themselves during the second half of the first year. Babies will cling to caregivers, cry, or hide their faces when they had previously accepted any attentive adult. Sometimes this behavior is viewed as a sign of stubbornness when in reality it is a sign of the emergence of self-protective instincts.

In the same way that young infants gradually recognize familiar people, they also come to accept and rely on a recognizable environment and daily routine. Disruption of environment and routine is especially stressful for babies in the first part of the second year, when a new environment or a change in parental work schedules may wreak havoc with a baby's sense of well-being.

Separation anxiety appears in connection with the cognitive skill of object permanence. The infant is suddenly aware that he has been abandoned by a familiar adult. He may call out or cry to an adult if he feels frightened or lonely. Again, this is a healthy turn of events. Erik Erikson states that the growth of basic trust is an essential task of infancy. The baby is signaling that he wants and expects favored adults to return to him, and each time this occurs he is rewarded by the continued growth of his idea that he is a loved and cared-for being, worthy of the attention of others.

Lacking the capacity to verbalize needs, the very young infant uses his body and cry to communicate with adults. However, patterns of early communication begin even in the first few months. First sounds, called cooing, consist of vowel-like noises usually produced when the baby is comfortable and alert. By six months of age, babies' communications are called babbling. These are vowel and consonant sounds run together. Until the end of the first year these noises are not generally meaningful; that is, the baby does not make them to produce true conversation. The sounds are basically random.

By ten months of age infants become capable of understanding simple commands and questions. They are by no means able to respond like older children to adult speech but they do indicate awareness when adults say, "Where is Daddy?" or "Go get your blanket."

First words are generally spoken around twelve months of age. At first infants use no sentences, just one word utterances. By the second birthday they are combining words into simple sentences and have a vocabulary of several hundred words. They may talk or sing to themselves and enjoy chattering to familiar adults, although not all of their speech may be intelligible. They may pick several words and frequently repeat them in a singsong or whiny voice.

Significance of Infant Behavior for Caregivers

Earlier we spoke of the significance of the infant's fitting into her environment. This fit is significant in several ways. It must first be achieved with caretaking adults who accept the infant as an individual. Some parents and caregivers come into conflict with infants whose behavior is perceived to be very different from their own. Adults sometimes think babies can be molded in their own image. When this does not happen—when there is a significant gap between the personality of the caregiver and that of the infant—problems can erupt. For example, an outgoing parent with a shy, introverted infant may feel a lack of connection to her baby. It is essential that from birth babies be perceived as unique beings with special needs, feelings, and accompanying behaviors. Caretaking adults must learn to be as proud of differences as they are of similarities between themselves and the children.

The signals of distress given off by infants should not be seen as manipulative or aimed at controlling adult behavior. Many adults fear that being overly responsive to infants leads to spoiling. Adults *cannot* respond too frequently to a genuinely distressed baby. The comfort and support the caretaker provides assures the baby of ongoing care and nurturance that she cannot provide for herself.

The overall reading of infant signals is also a significant part of the adult–baby relationship. Young infants not only give off distress signals, they also indicate a desire to play and to "talk." Since any chance for adult–infant interaction is a learning opportunity, caregivers should not ignore the cooing and babbling sounds that are overtures to "play with me." Also, while babies do not literally talk, they do participate in synchronous conversation-type interactions with adults when provided with the opportunity. Later language skills are influenced by these experiences.

Despite pressures from parents and some so-called experts for early academic training for young children, most developmentalists remain convinced that play opportunities are essential throughout early childhood. For infants this means sensory experiences and adults who cuddle and talk to them. It means careful selection of toys and materials that stimulate and challenge them but do not overtire them or tax their interests. As infants gradually achieve locomotion they should be able to count on having a safe and interesting environment to explore, populated by grown-ups who encourage them and explain what they are encountering. Some of the earliest "problem" behaviors occur when children explore in hazardous or unsafe areas, injuring themselves or damaging adults' treasures.

In the course of their explorations of the environment infants encounter a variety of exciting and sometimes frightening stimuli. Barking dogs, racing fire engines, clattering trains, and other experiences can cause babies to cling and cry. Similarly, trips to new places, the zoo, the supermarket, the park, and first times at a day care center can cause infants to exhibit the signs of separation anxiety. Unfortunately, many adults view such behaviors as inappropriate. Americans value bravery and resourcefulness even in their infants. A male infant who cries and clings may be seen as a sissy or as effeminate. (On the other hand, a female infant may actually be encouraged to be fearful.) It should be remembered that fear reactions are normal in babies under even mildly stressful circumstances. Infants should be supported, calmed, and never pushed into situations that are clearly fear producing. With adult encouragement babies learn to enjoy exploration of the world and gradually to appreciate encounters with new people.

Developmental Changes in Toddlerhood

Although the months eighteen to thirty-six are usually considered the toddler times, this phase actually begins as soon as the child becomes mobile. For some infants that may be as early as nine months. Once first steps are accomplished children are usually toddling, then rapidly running about in no time at all. Many adults consider the toddler years the most difficult in childhood. The often placid, easily controlled infant is replaced by a child who seems bent on self-destruction and sometimes on destruction of property as well.

Without question this is a challenging period, but the reasons that it is so difficult may surprise some caregivers. This is, above all, a frustrating time for the child. While he has acquired a set of basic skills, he has neither the sophistication or patience to use them like an older child does. He is constantly confronted and confounded by adult language, adult environments, and adult rules. He wants to participate in the exciting world around him, but adults constantly prevent him from doing so. In fits of rage and despair he screams, he bites, he throws himself on the floor. He is, in a word, impossible to deal with.

Physical Growth and Toddler Behavior

The toddler has a very specific appearance. His face and body are round. His limbs, including fingers, are short and fat. His legs are bowed. Therefore, the toddler is often clumsy. His belly is round and protrudes. His head appears larger than the rest of his body, and when running it pulls his torso slightly forward. While this child is able to walk, his gait is still unsteady. He bumps into objects and falls down easily.

Handling objects is difficult for the toddler. The small muscles of his hands are poorly developed so that he has difficulty with dressing, feeding skills, and other fine-motor activities. Spills at the table are common, often to the chagrin of caregivers and parents.

Toddlers also develop peculiar eating habits. They often eat constantly and more or less indiscriminately. With a consistently high level of energy and a rapidly growing body, calories are burned quickly and need to be replenished by frequent, small meals. Sometimes toddlers' activity seems aimless as they move quickly from one thing to the next.

With boundless energy and curiosity toddlers tackle the world around them but they need adult guidance and support to accomplish this safely. If adults prepare an environment designed to safeguard children's well-being, then they also prevent countless child behavior problems. Toddlers are unable to make judgments about the safety of their activities, and they rely on adults to anticipate their movements and interests.

Cognitive Growth and Toddler Behavior

By age two toddlers have acquired an entirely new set of concepts and cognitive skills. Although still egocentric, their ability to think symbolically has emerged in the form of early attempts at dramatic play and rapidly developing language. Symbolic thought refers to the ability to create mental images. When a toddler asks for a cookie, he clearly knows which food he is requesting. A toddler also recognizes adult activities and responds accordingly. For example, on hearing a caregiver say, "Do you want to go outside?" he runs to get his coat and begins dressing to go outside.

Toddlers also pick up and repeat many adult expressions without necessarily grasping their meaning. The extremely rapid vocabulary growth is a normal aspect of toddler and preschool development. A common complaint of caregivers concerns toddlers' use of bad words. Toddlers may use terms like *stupid* or *shut up* and may even adopt these words as a part of their vocabulary for a time. Unfortunately, these words are usually learned from primary caregivers. Adults hearing them from toddlers for the first time, often find them cute or amusing. On observing the initial adult response, the child feels rewarded and soon repeats the behavior.

A developing interest in dramatic play is another indicator of the emergence of symbolic thought. While infants will dial a toy telephone and carry a baby doll as an adult does, toddlers' play takes a distinctly different form as they begin to role-play a variety of adult activities. At first this play revolves around mother–child interactions. It eventually assumes more complex forms. Still, toddlers are capable of pretending to cook at a toy stove, shop for groceries, talk on the telephone, and care for a baby, to name a few common themes.

Animism is also a characteristic of toddler thought. It refers to young child's tendency to attribute human characteristics to animals or nonliving things. Thus, the toddler can believe that cartoon and movie characters are as real as he is. He believes quite literally that animals live, dress, and talk as people do. Santa Claus, the Easter Bunny, and the Tooth Fairy are as real to the toddler as his parents are.

Yet sometimes toddlers' belief in the world of fantasy creates problems for them. Unable to separate what is real from what is pretend, they believe in the influences of mythologic creatures, animals, ghosts, and witches on their world. They become very frightened when they feel threatened by the images and ideas they are capable of imagining and are probably unable to explain their fears to others. Bigger than real life, these fears may crowd out everything else. Some children even become emotionally immobilized. Some fears create nightmares or seemingly unreasonable responses to harmless stimuli. Consider the following real-life situation and how a caregiver might appropriately respond to it:

> A preschool teacher visited a toddler from his classroom at the child's home. During his visit the teacher planned to teach a demonstration lesson related to dressing and naming articles of clothing. Toward this end the teacher had made a large paper doll with movable limbs connected by paper fasteners and with a variety of articles of clothing. After introducing the lesson to the toddler and her parent, the teacher removed the doll from his bag. When the child saw the doll he took one look at it and began screaming, pointing at the doll, and saying, "No, no!"

Select the appropriate response to this situation from those listed below. Carefully consider the reasons for your choice.

    a. Ask the toddler to tell you what is wrong and why the doll is so frightening.

    b. Ask the child's mother to explain the behavior.

    c. Ask the toddler's mother to get her child under control so you can proceed with the lesson.

    d. Put the doll away, comfort the child, and begin another activity.

If you recall what we have said about the causes of fears and the toddler's inability to express them you probably correctly selected d. This is not the time to question the child. This is certainly not the time to force the child to participate in the activity. The child needs to be comforted and distracted. At some later point he may be more amenable to a discussion about his fears.

It is important for adults to accept that the young child's thinking is dramatically different from that of adults. You cannot simply give the child a rational explanation or teach the child to think differently. Only continued development will make the changes in the child's perceptions and concepts. Caregivers need to understand how children think so that the caregivers can determine appropriate responses to their behaviors.

Psychosocial Development and Toddler Behavior

While there are many unique aspects of the toddler's social and emotional development, a prominent feature of this phase is an offshoot of egocentrism. The toddler does not recognize needs other than his own, nor does he understand that gratifying his needs may be dependent on circumstances, events, or people. Thus, when he decides that he is hungry, thirsty, tired, or needs the restroom, he expects that need to be addressed immediately. He cannot delay gratification of those needs and if required to do so for too long a period he may cry or scream in frustration or even take matters into his own hands.

The toddler personality is generally an odd mixture of dependence and independence. Clinging and cuddly at one moment, the toddler may be yelling "No" a minute later. Abrupt mood swings are common, as are frequent needs for reassurance. Because the toddler is striving toward a measure of independence, opportunities to practice independent behaviors are necessary. An environment that nurtures and promotes development during this phase has two key elements. First, it has a dependable daily schedule, where changes are announced well in advance and are prepared for by adults and children. Second, by design it should encourage age-appropriate choices. Limits are clearly set; freedoms are easily identified. Thus, the environment itself limits the frustrations encountered by the toddler.

The most important aspect of the psychosocial growth encountered in the toddler years is that of autonomy. Everything about this child's behavior points to his need for independence and the first gentle break from the symbiotic parent–child relationship. For the first months of life the baby thinks of himself as a part of his mother. As a toddler, he begins to see himself as a separate person with interests and needs that do not always coincide with those of his parents. Attitudinal changes are accompanied by new physical independence (running and walking) and skills, such as learning to feed himself and use the toilet. Each new accomplishment is a triumph for the child. It is essential that caregiving adults recognize and praise these achievements. The toddler measures his successes by the degree of praise offered by adults. If the verbal rewards are lavish, the child's autonomy grows. But if his successes are ignored or his failures are too harshly criticized, then, Erikson tells us, shame and self-doubt develop.

The biggest challenge for adults who care for toddlers is accepting that this child is no longer controllable in the same sense that the infant was. The adult must, at some point, even welcome the toddler's new-found independence if the child is to develop to full potential. As we will discuss in the next section, the secondary challenge for caregivers is to create guidelines and a structure in which the toddler can function.

During the toddler years language enters into a period of rapid development lasting through most of early childhood. Words are picked up quickly and indiscriminately from adult conversations, from other children, and from television. Children still have difficulty with pronunciation, and not all terms and metaphors are familiar or understandable to them. They may talk nonstop around parents and become quiet as mice near strange adults or unfamiliar children. Favorite words may include *what, why,* and *no.* Children are still not truly conversational in the toddler years, and monologues are common. Some adults find the toddler's inability to converse or to follow all directions frustrating. However, it is important to remember that the toddler also becomes frustrated by his inability to express himself when he wants his needs met. That frustration often results in angry crying or tantrums.

Significance of Toddler Behavior for Caregivers

Caring for toddlers in a home or classroom setting can be a joyous experience. They are lively, vitally interested in the world around them, and extremely loving and affectionate when attached to an adult. However, they are passing through a challenging phase of development. Their insecurities are easily triggered, and when upset or frightened their behavior may become regressive. They may act like infants. So a critical job for caregivers and teachers is to create an environment that is safe, healthy, and very secure. The greater the toddler's sense of security, the fewer her emotional ups and downs will be. This end is accomplished through a variety of means, including the behaviors of adults involved, the physical setting, and the daily routine. The exercise "Making the Connection Between Toddler Behavior and Safety," provided here, offers some examples of ways to create a safe environment for toddlers and some of the behavioral problems avoided by use of these techniques.

Providing Consistency

Infants and toddlers are most secure when the same adults care for them on a daily basis. The concept of having "primary" caretakers is one found throughout the literature on parent–child attachment and has recently been applied in nursing and day care. Children respond well to having the same adult caregivers each day. These adults handle and care for the child's needs on a daily basis. They respond to the child in a consistent manner, helping the child know what to expect from the world and providing an example on which the young child can base her own responses.

Just as young children need consistency from adult caregivers, they also need it from the environment or setting in which they are cared for. The environment must be one of stability, with rare and gradual changes. For example, if one wanted to rearrange the day care setting where babies and toddlers are cared for, one should ideally do it before a new group of children begins attending the program. If changes must be undertaken when there is an established group of children, it is best to make them early in the day when the children are present, thereby giving them an entire day to become adjusted. Changes should not be made during the evening or over the weekend.

The third area that should provide consistency for the young child is that of the daily routine. The toddler period is one in which reliance on day-to-day activities is important. The child usually responds poorly to a change in meal times, rest times, or play times. Furthermore, if toilet training is a part of caregiving, the child must be taken to the potty chair or toilet at the same times each day. This does not mean that activities cannot be varied, but even the activities should fall within a group of familiar themes, like sand and water play, block play, housekeeping play, and the like. Very young children are most comfortable when the daily routine is as dependable as their adult caregivers.

For a summary of developmental milestones in the infant and toddler phases, see the outline provided, "Developmental Milestones in Infancy and Toddlerhood."

Developmental Changes in Preschool Children

The years from three through five are a fun and exciting time for children and the adults around them. Many of the behaviors that adults associate with toddlerhood have disappeared. Children of this age are more verbal

Making the Connection between Toddler Behavior and Safety

A safe environment for play and exploration is one that also minimizes inappropriate behavior in toddlers. It removes opportunities for disruptive and destructive activity that may also be harmful to the child. The exploring toddler does not always see her behavior as harmful or difficult. Driven by curiosity and imagination, she touches, tastes, and smells whatever interests her. During this developmental phase the perception of behaviors as inappropriate usually comes from an adult who must cope with the consequences of the child's explorations.

Directions: Below is a partial list of tips for safeguarding and child-proofing toddler environments. Use the space in the right-hand column to list the behavior problems that can be avoided through use of this safety tip. After completing the exercise, see if you can brainstorm to add additional safety tips to the list.

Example:

Safety Tip	Problem Avoided
• Remove collectibles from child's reach.	• Prevents toddlers from breaking adult's valuables.
• Provide storage space for toys not in use.	
• Remove or hide electrical/extension cords from child's view.	
• Lock lower storage cabinets and/or remove all cleaning fluids and medicines from child's reach.	
• Provide child-sized equipment (tables, cots, chairs, toilets, sinks) wherever possible.	
• Put infant seats or seat belts in all vehicles used for transporting children.	

Developmental Milestones in Infancy and Toddlerhood

	Infancy (birth–18 months)	Toddlerhood (18 months–3 years)
Physical	• Newborn has reflexive behaviors (crying, sucking, grasping, startling) • Young infant may experience periods of inconsolability due to colic or sensory overload • As large muscles develop, infant attempts to gain control of body	• Toddler has distinguishing physical characteristics (bowed legs, round face, etc.) • Toddler is physically clumsy • Toddler is very active • Toddler eats frequent meals
Cognitive	• Infant senses begin functioning in womb • Newborn does not recognize own impact on caretakers, environment • As infant learns of own ability to cause reaction she experiments to see if reactions are repeated • Infant is egocentric; recognizes only own needs • Infant begins to understand that objects out of sight continue to exist (object permanence)	• Toddler is rapidly developing new concepts (symbolic thought) • Toddler attributes characteristics of humans to nonhuman things (animism) • Toddler often cannot distinguish between reality and fantasy • Toddler continues to be egocentric

Developmental Milestones in Infancy and Toddlerhood
(continued)

	Infancy (Birth–18 Months)	**Toddlerhood** (18 Months–3 Years)
Psychosocial	• Infant does not initially differentiate between familiar and unfamiliar adults • Infant begins to distinguish parents from others • Infant reacts poorly to unfamiliar persons, environments (stranger anxiety) • Infant reacts poorly to separation from parents, caregivers (separation anxiety)	• Toddler responds best to consistency in caregivers, environment, routine • Toddler cannot delay gratification of basic needs • Toddler is at times very dependent, at times attempts independence • Toddler may have abrupt mood swings due to frustration • Toddler is very responsive to praise • Toddler may regress behaviorally when stressed
Language	• First sounds are reflexive • Infant coos as a form of communication (2 months) • Infant babbles to communicate (6 months) • Infant understands simple commands (10 months) • Infant speaks first words (12 months)	• Toddler spoken language acquisition rapid, but comprehension skills slower to develop • Toddler has difficulties with articulation

and usually more cooperative. They are physically capable of a broader range of activities and are easily entertained. They have generally lost their fear of strangers and animals. Friendly and outgoing, except under stressful circumstances, preschoolers enjoy new people and novel events.

Physical Growth and Preschooler Behavior

By age three the young child's growth rate has slowed appreciably from that which she experienced during the infant and toddler years. A steady rate of growth continues, but the physical changes are somewhat less noticeable during the years from three to five. However, the preschooler is easily distinguished from the toddler in appearance. The three-year-old is no longer bowlegged. Her head no longer seems too large for her body, and her gait is more steady, less awkward. She has better balance and coordination, and these skills steadily improve throughout this phase. She can hop, skip, balance briefly on one foot, and pedal a tricycle.

Her fine-motor abilities are somewhat less refined. Although this child feeds and dresses herself, fastening that button, snap, and zipper can be difficult. She cannot tie her shoes or use scissors with ease. Throughout this phase and into middle childhood her small muscles will continue their development.

Obvious external changes in the preschooler are accompanied by not so apparent internal differences. The stomach and bladder are larger and more stable. Therefore, there are fewer digestive and intestinal upsets. The immune system has developed further, and colds and flus diminish in number. The body temperature drops and finally stabilizes. The distance between the outer and inner ear lengthens, so ear infections are less frequent.

Although it is difficult for some adults to believe, most preschoolers are less physically active than toddlers. A reduction in activity and a slowing of the growth rate result in the need for fewer calories, so the child's appetite is usually diminished and less sleep is needed. Adults are often upset by the picky appetites of preschoolers. It is important for caregivers to recognize that this is a natural aspect of preschool development, and a healthy child will eat when hungry. Forcing a child to eat may cause digestive or elimination problems, or the child may become overweight.

Cognitive Growth and Preschooler Behavior

The period of intellectual growth from approximately two to seven years is called "preoperational" by Piaget. This period of cognition is characterized by the emergence of symbolic thought. The preoperational stage begins for many children around age two. Therefore, symbolic thought and other characteristics of preoperations may first appear in toddlers. The child has the capacity to mentally represent simple concepts and images. For example, she uses language to verbalize needs and wants. She can also act out the activities or roles of favorite persons or characters. All of these abilities require symbolic thought.

Other characteristics of this stage, many of which are also present in toddlers, include centration, egocentrism, and animism. Centration refers to the child's inability to think of more than one aspect or element of something at a time. Thus, the child may have trouble thinking of her mother as anything but her mother, despite the fact that her mother may be the daughter, sister, aunt, or cousin of others. Egocentrism is the child's tendency to see the world only from her own point of view. She believes that the world revolves around her and that people and nature act and react for her benefit. Animism causes children to believe that all creatures and objects think and behave as people do, and helps explain why young children can believe that Santa Claus, the Easter Bunny, and the Tooth Fairy are as real as people.

As preoperational thinkers, children may evaluate the speech and activities of adults differently than grown-ups intended. For instance, the young child believes that what adults say is meant literally, even when metaphors or figures of speech are used. These aspects of cognition in the preschool and early school-aged years can create misunderstandings and fears in the young child. Children require understanding and support from caregivers, who must recognize that only development and growth into the next period of cognition will change the child's thinking.

The accompanying exercise, "How Young Children Think," provides a way for you to assess your knowledge of cognitive development during the preschool years.

Psychosocial Development and Preschooler Behavior

Children are often significantly less fearful in the preschool years. They enjoy adults, other children, and familiar animals. They have developed independence to the degree that they can comfortably separate from adults to enjoy a day at preschool or a brief visit with grandparents. They are generally friendly and cooperative, especially when adults focus individualized attention on them. However, when tired or stressed sharing adult attention can be difficult for preschoolers. While able to play companionably alongside of other children, they may erupt into tears of anger when they feel thwarted.

Preschoolers demonstrate a growing range of dramatic play abilities. At first their games are limited to acting out household activities, such as shopping, cooking, or caring for babies. Gradually, however, they begin

How Young Children Think

Directions: Below you will find a list of things young children commonly say and do during the preoperational stage. Identify the cause of this behavior and label it as *egocentrism, animism, centration,* or *inability to understand metaphors.*

_____ 1. A child tells his mother that he has looked "around the corner" for Christmas but cannot find it.

_____ 2. A child says, "The sun shines to keep me warm."

_____ 3. On seeing a baby bird a child says, "Is he sad because he lost his mommy?"

_____ 4. While playing in the sand at the beach, a child says, "A hole is to dig."

_____ 5. A child searches her house for her mother's mind because, "You said you lost it."

_____ 6. A child touches a relative tentatively and says, "You're not cold. Mommy said you are cold."

_____ 7. While coloring a child insists that bears and chickens can be colored blue because they are "blue on television."

_____ 8. A child insists that her friend's German shepherd is not a dog, because her own pet (a collie) is not a dog.

Answer Key: 1. metaphors; 2. egocentrism; 3. animism; 4. egocentrism; 5. metaphors; 6. metaphors; 7. animism or centration; 8. centration

to explore other situations and roles, including those of cartoon superheroes, community helpers, or movie figures. They are able to play more cooperatively, including additional children and ideas in their games.

Erikson says that the preschooler is involved in developing initiative. She is growing in her self-awareness and knowledge of her impact on her environment. She is more willing to approach new situations but may not always realize the repercussions of her activities. When involved in an exciting activity she may become so involved that she forgets completely about going to the bathroom or about something her father told her to do.

The preschooler generally has strong feelings of self-esteem. She feels she is smarter, prettier, draws better, and runs faster than anyone else. Her good feelings about self are appropriate and should not be altered by adult opinions or introductions to the "real world." Adult praise should be frequent and lavish without concern for spoiling. The feelings the child develops about self in the preschool period are often those that last a lifetime.

The rapid language growth of the preschool years is due in part to the emergence of symbolic thought. From the two-hundred-word vocabulary of the second year, a child develops one of up to fourteen thousand words by age six. Even five-year-olds can learn almost any term as long as it is appropriately explained to them.

As mentioned, egocentrism and the concrete nature of children's thinking still affect their language in this stage. Words that describe emotions or abstract terms are hard for children to grasp. Figurative expressions or metaphors are confusing for preschoolers, and understanding of comparative terms like *near* and *far* may be influenced by centration. Here is an example of that confusion:

> A four-year-old boy sat at a table with his preschool teacher. She was using flashcards to teach him the names of articles of clothing. The cards showed shirts, shoes, dresses, pants, and hats without figures or bodies inside of them. When the teacher showed the boy the flashcard showing a long-sleeved shirt, she asked, "What is this? Do you see the collar? Do you see the sleeves?" Then she asked, "Are the sleeves long or short?" The boy knew the garment was a shirt. He knew the location of the collar and sleeves, but he said the sleeves were short. Why? Because he judged them by his size, not by their size in relation to the shirt.

Consider the following: Could an adult better explain the difference between short and long sleeves to the child by using the flashcards or by using a real shirt? Is the flashcard picture of a shirt the best way to learn about long and short? Remember, this child is a concrete learner. Also consider that some adults become angry when a child gives an "incorrect" response to a question with an answer that the adult feels is obvious.

This example illustrates the strong connection between cognition and language. Many concepts are learned through the language development opportunities provided by adults. Children use their senses to gather information, and with adult assistance learn to group and categorize their ideas into concepts with words used to express them.

Other language difficulties include overregularization—the tendency to overuse rules of grammar—and difficulty with pragmatics. An example of overregularization is adding -s or -ed to a word when instead a change in the form of the word would be appropriate, as in saying "sheeps" instead of "sheep." Adult attempts to explain or correct preschool children's speech are hampered by the fact that children's speech is influenced by their thinking. Only time and further development will change some patterns of speech, and scolding may make the child afraid to speak.

Significance of Preschooler Behavior for Caregivers

Promoting the growth of the preschooler's self-esteem is probably the most important role that adults can play during this period. In each aspect of his development, physical, cognitive, and psychosocial, the child strives toward new accomplishments and looks for support for his endeavors. He needs the same safe environment the toddler requires for exploration, but his challenges must be greater. He must be permitted more risks without fear of reprisals from adults. He must be allowed to make mistakes and to experience their consequences. Given these opportunities, he will gradually develop a more accurate self-concept.

The problem behaviors of the preschool years must be accepted as normal aspects of development. When children are whiny and uncooperative, and they refuse to share, there are generally good reasons for it, such as overstimulation, hunger, or tiredness. One way of cutting down on behavior problems is simply to avoid making unnecessary demands on children.

Preschoolers benefit from routines, just as toddlers do. Too many schedule and activity changes upset and frustrate them. Three-, four-, and five-year-olds also do better when the adults who care for them are consistent and dependable. Unlike toddlers, however, preschoolers have a greater capacity for learning and abiding by rules, provided the rules are simple and clear-cut, with well-established consequences. Young children need time to practice rules and understand their purposes. Writing the rules down and regularly reinforcing them is among the best ways to help them remember what is expected.

Finally, no young child should be expected to go for too long a period without some form of adult reinforcement. That may consist of one-on-one time, or may be as simple as a hug, smile, or pat. These are the signs that tell a child he is recognized and accepted as special by the grown-ups who care for him.

Developmental Changes in Middle Childhood

Sometimes called the school years, middle childhood begins with a child's entry into formal education in kindergarten or first grade. Although middle childhood lasts from age six until the onset of puberty, this book will address the child's development only up to age nine. This period is the advent of many new and sometimes frightening experiences for children, even when it is preceded by preschool. Middle childhood does have its compensations, however. It is a relatively stable period developmentally. And although a great deal of support is still available to children through home, school, and extracurricular activities, they have the capacity to begin to explore the world away from their parents. Under ideal circumstances children have the resources and support to explore a wider world and to begin to know themselves and their capabilities in relation to those around them.

Physical Growth in the Early School Years

The years from six through nine are ones of slow, steady growth. The child generally becomes proportionally thinner during these years. His heart grows stronger, and the vital capacity of his lungs increases. With increased muscle strength, he is gradually able to play and exercise for longer periods. As during all of childhood, heredity, ethnicity, nutrition, and overall health are also factors in physical maturation.

Perhaps for the first time children become conscious of their appearance, size, and shape. They compare themselves to other youngsters and may develop their first concerns about how they look. It is at this time that children are labeled as different by others and first experience the taunts of their peers. Different can mean many things, developmental differences or handicaps; too fat or too thin; too tall or too short.

Girls and boys tend to develop in very similar ways during middle

---

In this section the term *middle childhood* will be used to refer to the child's stage of development between six and nine years, and *school-age* will be used as a description of the child during the same period.

childhood. The differences are very slight and include greater forearm strength in boys and better balance and coordination in girls. An overriding factor in these aspects of development is, however, the individual child's experience and opportunities to practice these skills.

A great many skills improve during middle childhood. The typical school-aged child can ride a bicycle, roller skate, jump rope, swim, draw in proportion, use tools, sew, and print with accuracy and neatness. Many of the activities of school-aged children consist of opportunities they create to practice motor skills. Little league sports, play with dolls and action figures, crafts and hobbies, and video games are all examples of mastery play activities. Even the seemingly mindless pursuits of balancing oneself on a low wall or avoiding cracks in the sidewalk provide opportunities for developing coordination.

Unfortunately, many adults lack patience for the passion with which children can sometimes devote themselves to their games. At a time when parents and some caregivers feel that children should be devoting themselves to schoolwork and academic pursuits, the children's interests generally lie elsewhere. Video games, baseball or soccer, scouting, and gymnastics are activities that can challenge and improve children's physical abilities.

Cognitive Growth in Middle Childhood

In the early years of middle childhood children are still preoperational thinkers. Their thinking skills are still very much like those of preschoolers. They are constrained by their egocentrism, centration, animism, and other aspects of preoperational thought. In the seventh or eighth year, however, a gradual shift to concrete operations, the third of Piaget's stages, begins. Children gradually begin to understand new concepts and simple abstract ideas, and egocentrism lessens. They are also able to make classifications, dividing objects into groups or categories. This ability becomes even more sophisticated with the development of class inclusion, a more complicated concept in which the child recognizes that objects may belong to more than one group.

Concepts of time and distance develop as the terms used in their measurement become more meaningful. However, for some time children will still have difficulty unraveling word problems that involve a combination of time, speed, and distance.

One of the main features of concrete operations is the emergence of conservation skills. Children understand basic principles of logic that assist them in the analysis of problems of length, volume, distance, area, and so on. As long as problems can be approached concretely children at the concrete operational level can tackle them. When problems require less concrete and more abstract skills the school-aged child usually cannot resolve them.

Adults probably question the child's thinking skills most when it comes to setting priorities and tackling everyday chores and homework. What seems like common sense to grown-ups is often based on many years of problem-solving and trial-and-error experiences. What an adult considers to be common sense may seem neither important nor practical to a school-aged child. "Why didn't you think?" is a question often asked by frustrated parents and teachers. The child did think, but not as an adult.

Psychosocial Development in Middle Childhood

Erikson calls the middle years the stage of "industry vs. inferiority." It is an early stage of productivity, of quiet energy. For the first time children take stock of themselves as they measure themselves against the rest of the world. It is the first time that the trust, autonomy, and initiative of the earlier years are put to the test. Furthermore, the self-esteem developed earlier in childhood helps children evaluate themselves realistically and face the disappointments that come with competition in the real world. As children grow in self-understanding, they are more likely to become self-critical and to blame themselves for failures.

Along with self-understanding comes additional understanding of others. In middle childhood children develop their first real friendships, beginning to share activities and confidences with others, although social activities are often sex segregated. Children begin to describe and rate the traits and personalities of others, and they begin to imagine themselves in terms of what they would like to be as adults. School-aged children put a great deal of energy into the mastery of their sex roles. Their behaviors may be exaggerated at times, and they may show a distaste for the behaviors of the opposite sex ("Boys are yucky!" or "Girls are gross!"). Interaction between the sexes often takes the form of chase games and teasing.

Friendships in middle childhood are often founded on "what the other person can do for me." Common reasons for selecting a friend are "He invites me over to his house," "His parents take us to the arcade," or "She has lots of sleepovers." However, children also judge their friends to be "nice," "pretty," and "funny." Friendships may change quickly and for reasons not always apparent to adults. A popular child can quickly become unpopular. A child's agreement to take a "dare" may make him a temporary hero to others. Children may lie, steal, or cheat to get or keep a friend. They will risk adult disapproval or even punishment to avoid the criticism of peers, as to them few punishments are worse than being held up to the ridicule of peers. Sometimes as quickly as children are angry, their friendships are restored, only to become embattled on another day.

You can test your knowledge of peer interactions in the early school years with the quiz, "Peer Relations in Middle Childhood."

Communication skills are well developed by middle childhood. This is a period when children first begin to enjoy and play with language. Telling jokes (even bathroom jokes), riddles, secrets, learning poems, and telling stories are all facets of that enjoyment. Children's use of name calling and verbal taunts as a mechanism for getting back at enemies is another aspect of language development in middle childhood.

One of the improvements in language skills during middle childhood is in the area of pragmatics. Children learn to modify their vocabulary and sentences and to use nonverbal clues in a variety of social situations. Code-switching skills also develop, enabling children to move from restricted to elaborate forms of speech depending on the setting or situation. Some forms of language used in middle childhood may be offensive to adults. Cursing may develop as a way to imitate grown-ups or to attract the attention of peers. This must be handled in the ways that are best suited to the child and the situation. The school-aged child is still influenced by adult opinions and is capable of learning that some language is simply unwelcome in social settings.

Significance of Middle Childhood Behaviors for Caregivers

In some ways middle childhood is an ideal developmental period. Children enjoy peers and in many ways are independent, yet still crave adult companionship and approval. They are prone to negative peer influences yet desire to please adults even more.

One key to promoting healthy development lies in encouraging independent behavior and choices appropriate to the child's developmental level. While many children protest the necessary imposition of adult rules, and some whine and cry, their acting-out behavior is usually short-lived.

School-aged children genuinely enjoy conversations with adults and are most responsive to those adults who are good listeners and indicate respect for the child's opinions and interests. When conflicts arise, children of this age can often be reasoned with. They are concerned about and generally responsive to adult needs and concerns when these are openly expressed. Problems often arise, however, when adults prove untrustworthy. Children take very seriously the claims and promises of their parents and teachers. If those adults are dishonest or fail to keep promises,

Peer Relations in Middle Childhood

Directions: The behaviors of school-aged children are often guided by the responses of their peers. Some of these behaviors are considered inappropriate by adults. It is helpful in guiding children if we understand the rationale for their behavior. Read each statement and select the appropriate answer from the choices provided.

1. Primary school-aged children (do/do not) understand the consequences of lying or stealing.

2. Repetitious activities, such as video games and skateboarding (do/do not) benefit a child's development.

3. Competition in school or extra-curricular activities (is/is not) helpful to the child's development of sense of self.

4. A child's self-image (is/is not) influenced by the opinions of peers during middle childhood.

5. Primary school-aged children may seem irresponsible in relation to parental expectations because their priorities are (the same/different) from those of adults.

6. In middle childhood children are generally (comfortable/uncomfortable) with sex-integrated activities.

7. Primary school-aged children (are/are not) likely to be very self-critical.

8. Children (do/do not) begin keeping things secret from adults in middle childhood.

9. Daring another child to perform a risky task (is/is not) one of the criteria for friendship in middle childhood.

10. Taunts and name calling (are/are not) forms of retribution in middle childhood.

© 1992 by The Center for Applied Research in Education

Answer Key: 1. do not; 2. do; 3. is; 4. is; 5. different; 6. uncomfortable; 7. are; 8. do; 9. is; 10. are

Developmental Milestones in the Preschool and Middle Years

	Preschool Years (3–5)	Early Middle Childhood (6–9)
Physical	• Preschooler's rate of overall growth slows • Preschooler's balance and coordination improve • Preschooler's small-muscle skills are still developing • Preschooler's digestive and elimination systems stabilize slowly • Preschooler's appetite is somewhat diminished	• Child's growth is slow but steady • Child's muscle strength increases • Boys have greater forearm strength • Girls have better coordination • Child's small-muscle strength increases
Cognitive	• Preschooler continues to be egocentric • Preschooler can consider only one aspect or element of something at a time (centration) • Preschooler takes adult speech literally	• Child may still have preoperational characteristics: centration, animism, egocentrism • Child gradually understands simple abstract concepts • Child develops ability to classify • Concepts of space, time, distance develop • Child becomes a conserver with entry into concrete operations

Developmental Milestones in the Preschool and Middle Years (continued)

	Preschool Years (3–5)	Early Middle Childhood (6–9)
Psychosocial	• Preschooler has fewer fears	• Child becomes conscious of own appearance
	• Preschooler is gradually able to play cooperatively, to sometimes share, wait for turn	• Child measures own abilities against those of others.
	• Preschooler's self-awareness is growing	• Child's social activities are usually sex segregated
	• Preschooler generally has good self-esteem	• Child's first real friendships develop but are usually egocentric in nature
	• Preschooler needs praise and support from adults	
Language	• Preschooler experiences most rapid period of language development	• Child's communication skills are well developed
	• Preschooler does not always understand metaphors	• Child comprehends and can tell secrets, jokes, riddles
	• Preschooler has difficulty with comparative terms	• Child's use of language is sometimes appropriate, sometimes inappropriate
	• Preschooler may incorrectly use word endings (overregularization)	

then children often become angry and rebellious. Still, the early school years can be a pleasant and happy time in many adult–child relationships. For a summary of milestones during the preschool years and middle childhood, see the outline provided.

In this chapter we described some of the many behaviors typical of children during early childhood. The purpose was to describe what is normal, not what is problematic. Our premise is simple: By far, most of children's behavior is normal. If demands are reasonable, environments are suitable, and adult responses are simple and direct, then misbehavior can be minimized or eliminated in most children.

chapter three

CLASSROOM MANAGEMENT FOR BETTER BEHAVIOR

When children annoy or frustrate us, we have a tendency to look for outside sources of the problem. We might blame the child's upbringing or seek the answer in an undiagnosed health problem. Sometimes we blame the child. Although it may be easier to look elsewhere than to blame ourselves for problems, we are sometimes very much at fault. Most of us do not deliberately provoke children into misbehavior. In fact, most of the inappropriate management techniques used by teachers are entirely well meaning. However, with the wrong information or misplaced priorities adults can create a wide range of problems among children.

In this chapter we will examine how significant adults, specifically teachers and caregivers, influence children's behavior. We will also describe some of the techniques that can be used by adults to promote positive behavior in children.

Adults as Role Models and Tone Setters

Our knowledge of child development enables us to understand that the very young child is most influenced by her parents and other primary caretakers. We see this influence in a wide variety of ways but none more significant than in the child's behavior. Young children imitate influential adults during dramatic play, in conversation, and in their interactions with other children. Children use us as a model for their language, for nurturing behaviors, and for their interpersonal skills. Even when we think she is not paying attention, the young child is watching us closely. Children are especially observant of us when we interact with other adults. If we use appropriate language, tact, and courtesy, children tend to do likewise. If on the other hand we are inconsiderate, ill mannered, or foulmouthed, children will pick up these behaviors. They can notice even the most subtle nuances in adult behavior. How often have you heard a parent ask of his preschooler, "I wonder where she picked up that behavior?" She generally picks it up from some important adult in her life.

Those who conduct research on leadership have been studying the impact of various styles of authority for many years. One of the roles of leaders is that of tone setter. This is an intangible sort of skill but one whose results are felt, as well as seen, in the classroom. Teachers and other adults present indicate through their voices, body language, and even their dress what the mood or tone of the classroom is.

An adult's loud, shrill, or scolding voice can set the tone. All adults occasionally become annoyed with children. However, if the adult constantly reprimands them, children may become worried or withdrawn. Once they become fearful of a scolding they are more likely to have instances of problems or disruptive behaviors. Consider what happens to adults when someone or something makes us nervous; we make mistakes, often the very ones we are trying to avoid. The same thing happens to young children.

Children are also influenced by an adult's facial expressions or body language. Good behavior is often a matter of how relaxed children are. If adults convey an uptight or stiff demeanor, children can quickly become ill at ease, worried about what the adult is thinking or feeling and what will happen next. Even small infants are sensitive to such things as shown by the way they will cry in response to a certain tone of voice.

Appropriateness of adult dress can influence the tone of the classroom. Surprisingly, many early childhood educators "dress to impress"; that is, they are more concerned about how parents or co-workers see them than about how their mode of dress affects their interactions with children. If we visit a school and see teachers or caregivers dressed as if for church or a dinner date we know immediately that there is a limit to what they can or will do with children. The child who is told, "Please, don't get paint on Miss Smith's skirt," receives a message about the importance of her work. Never should an adult imply by her dress, "I simply cannot get down on the floor with you or I will muss up my clothing." By the way, parents can easily misinterpret the meaning of the fancy dress of teachers. They may mistakenly assume that children should be similarly dressed. This can lead to all manner of home–school problems due to the soiling of children's expensive clothing.

The language of the teacher can also set the tone. A teacher's language does not have to be foul to be inappropriate. Consider, for instance, the use of nonstandard English. Neither children nor their parents expect school or day care to be exactly like home. One thing most parents expect and most children need is a language model. They want and need teachers to demonstrate for their children the speech that is acceptable in school and work settings. The teacher's home or neighborhood speech should not be her professional language, even though each type has its place. (Consider the case of the preschooler who came home crying because his teacher said that his outfit was "bad." The child thought that the teacher had said that he was bad, while she had been paying him a compliment.) Use of academic jargon can be similarly harmful. An unnecessary barrier may be set up between teachers and parents or teachers and children by language that is too formal or foreign. While it is true that we learn special vocabulary in conjunction with our work with young children, most of that language was designed to enhance our communication with one another. Using academic jargon with parents or children who are unfamiliar with it can cause confusion, resentment, and anger. We may seem to be deliberately excluding them from participating in a conversation with us.

Part of setting a positive tone also comes from the way caregivers interact with children's parents. If parents are made to feel comfortable about the caregiver and the classroom, this comfort is transferred to the children. A parent who is at ease is more likely to leave the caregiver with a happy and contented child, who has fewer behavior problems.

What Is Good Child Behavior?

Sadly, we are not far removed from a time when the "good child" was "seen but not heard." In fact, many teachers of young children still believe and adhere to this old adage. Adults often measure the quality of a child's behavior by the degree to which he is polite, neat, orderly, and quiet. If we examine these notions, however, we find that the young child often has difficulty measuring up to adult standards. Most young children are noisy, messy, rude, and disorderly on occasion. The idea of the unobtrusive child is an outmoded one, stemming from beliefs that children think like adults and are, therefore, capable of behaving like adults. These qualities are measures made according to adult norms. They are not standards that should apply to an early childhood educator's expectations for children. Perhaps we cling to these older notions because they are what we know best, but they are not in the best interests of the child.

When we closely examine what is developmentally normal for the young child (see Chapter Two), we realize that age characteristics, like centration and egocentrism, interfere with the child's ability to think and perform at an adult level. When it comes to appropriate behavior, the child's attention is often focused elsewhere. An ardent explorer of his environment, fascinated by all that his senses reveal, the child does not focus on politeness when there is a question to be asked.

Are we suggesting that it is wrong to have expectations for children or to teach children manners? No, indeed. However, what we do suggest is that if adults think of young children as being easily able to develop adult behaviors, then those expectations are inappropriate. How can the young child be expected to observe social convention when he has no basis for comprehending our requests and is drawn to other interests? Children *can* gradually acquire manners and become neat and orderly, but only if adults are patient and understanding, introducing rules in age-appropriate ways. In the meantime, we must be aware that children will continue to interrupt our conversations, forget to replace toys, and hit other children. It is, after all, what children do. If adult expectations are reasonable, children are less likely to disappoint us, to fall into the "bad child" trap that we sometimes set for them. Check your knowledge of the "good child" by completing the quiz, "Do You Recognize Children's Normal Behaviors?"

Rewarding Inappropriate Behavior

Adults sometimes create problems for young children by rewarding the wrong behaviors. On many occasions the authors have observed circle time or some large-group activity in a preschool classroom, and watched an adult interrupt the work of all other children to reprimand one uncooperative child. This action on the part of the teacher suggests many things to those children who are cooperative. For example, it suggests that the work of most of the class is less important than the activity of the disruptive child, because the teacher's attention to this behavior says so. It also suggests that one effective way to get the teacher's attention is to misbehave, because the teacher's response to this behavior says so. While these are not the messages the teacher intends to give, they are, nonetheless, often the ones received by the children who observe the teacher's behavior.

Perhaps you are asking, "What am I supposed to do, ignore the disruptive child?" In some cases, yes! Let us examine two possible scenarios.

Scenario I

You are reading a story to a group of children; most are engrossed. About halfway through the story one child begins to fidget. She gets up and begins

Do You Recognize Children's Normal Behaviors?

Directions: Read each statement carefully. Consider whether the behavior described is "normal" or inappropriate. After making your choice of these two place either an "N" or a "B" in the space provided. Check your answers below. Remember to consider what you know about children's development.

_____ 1. A four-year-old child tells a fantastic story about his experiences with a dinosaur.

_____ 2. A three-year-old child cries for a long time when her mother leaves her at day care.

_____ 3. A three-year-old boy cries when another child takes his toy bear.

_____ 4. A two-year-old "takes" another toddler's doll.

_____ 5. A three-year-old girl leaves the preschool playground because she says she sees her mother's bus coming.

_____ 6. A two-year-old bites another toddler.

_____ 7. A nine-month-old infant "slaps" her mother.

_____ 8. A five-year-old calls her friend a name when they have a fight.

_____ 9. A four-year-old says "Damn!" when he falls down.

_____ 10. An eighteen-month-old cries to be picked up.

Answer Key: None of these behaviors is inappropriate. All are normal for the age level identified. While not all of the above behaviors are desirable in a child, the adult responsible for discipline should consider how that behavior has been influenced or caused by the child's level of development.

to wander quietly around the room. Eventually, she selects a puzzle, sits at a table, and begins putting it together. What is your role?

Choice A: You tell the child to put away the puzzle and come back to the group immediately.
Choice B: You ignore the child, even if another child joins her.

If you selected B, good for you. You realize that the distraction created by your calling to the child would be greater than any she created by leaving the group. Try scenario 2.

Scenario 2

You are reading to the children. One child is restless from the outset. He quickly wanders away from the group and to the block area. There he begins to stack blocks noisily and sing to himself. What is your role?

Choice A: You tell the child to stop the noise and return to the group.
Choice B: You ignore the child.
Choice C: You say quietly, "Brian, please play quietly so that the other children can hear the story."

If you chose C you probably already have a smooth-running class-room. Since Brian was being disruptive, you had little choice except to intervene. However, you did it in the least disruptive way possible, and you did not reward Brian. You merely asked him to respect the learning time of the other children.

There are times, of course, when teachers and caregivers must inter-vene to stop children's inappropriate behaviors. This is especially true when a child's safety is at stake. Stopping the behavior may also mean punishing it. Later in this book we will explore exactly what appropriate punishment entails. In the meantime, complete the checklist "Do You Reward Inappropriate Behavior?"

The Controlling Teacher

More than two decades ago, the concept of child-centeredness was intro-duced into the early childhood curriculum. In theory, this notion suggests that children themselves can set the directions for learning. By staying in tune with developmental needs and interests, the teacher follows the lead of the children in planning the program. In early childhood class-rooms this concept has been translated into features like interest centers and free-choice time. However, it sometimes seems that many of us missed the point. What was intended by John Dewey and other twenti-eth-century proponents of the open classroom was that adults understand

Do You Reward Inappropriate Behavior?

Directions: Each time a child behaves inappropriately adults make a choice about how to respond. Below are some sample behaviors commonly seen among young children, accompanied by potential adult reactions. Select the response that you think is least likely to reward this behavior.

1. While talking to one child another approaches you and interrupts, calling your name. You should:
   a. stop talking to the first child and talk to the second.
   b. ignore the interrupter.
   c. ask the interrupter to wait, then continue talking to the first child.

2. During clean-up time one child begins pulling blocks off the shelf after others have just put them away. You should:
   a. ignore the behavior.
   b. go to the child and help her put the blocks back.
   c. ask the children who are finished cleaning up to get ready for outdoor play.

3. When she wants a turn on a tricycle, a child pushes a rider off. You should:
   a. remove the child from the tricycle and give her a time out.
   b. let her take her turn on the tricycle.
   c. ignore the behavior.

4. A child tears up another child's artwork. You should:
   a. praise her artwork since she obviously feels bad.
   b. tell her not to damage another's work, and ask her to apologize.
   c. tear up her art work.

5. A child has brought candy to school although it is against the class rules. She cries when you take it from her. You should:
   a. give her the candy.
   b. tell her she can take it home with her at the end of the day.
   c. throw the candy away.

Answer Key: 1. c; 2. c; 3. a; 4. b; 5. b

that children can, do, and should make choices in the classroom if learning is to take place.

Often, when visiting early childhood centers, the authors see free-choice time interpreted in this way:

> "You may pick one of the interest centers, Johnny. Oh, you selected blocks. I'm sorry. The block area is closed. No, housekeeping area is closed, too. The art area is open, why not play there. I'm sorry, Johnny, the Play Doh® is off limits today. You can choose from the finger paint or the easel. What *is* that, Johnny? Oh, it's a tree. But Johnny, trees are not purple."

What all of this has to do with the influence of teachers on children's behavior is very simple. Children need freedom to explore, to be creative, to discover without adult interference. Poor Johnny had very little of that. Is it any wonder that he wound up smearing the paint on the floor and sliding around in it?

It would be naive of us to suggest that we don't to some degree measure good teaching by the amount of authority a teacher exerts over his pupils, but what does this "control" mean to many teachers? It often means that we plan and account for every move that every child makes; that we cut off opportunities for spontaneity by planning every minute, even to the point of having a set of anticipated responses that children should make. We do not have any surprises in the classroom because we fear that surprises will lead to disruption, which in turn will lead to chaotic behavior.

What impact does this rigidity have on the children? The young child, ready and eager for the unanticipated, can easily begin to feel caged. The child who feels locked into a set of rigidly determined activities and responses to them may seek anything novel so he can experience some stimulation—even to the point of engaging in the forbidden and the dangerous.

The authors once observed a teacher working with a group of toddlers. She had planned an activity designed to promote the children's recognition of the names of facial parts (nose, mouth, eyes). Incorporating a Valentine's Day theme, the teacher made the faces and facial parts in the shape of hearts. However, trouble erupted when one child reached into the plastic bag that held the heart features for another "nose." The teacher grabbed the bag, exclaiming. "You already have a nose. You don't need another one." Dissolving into tears, the toddler threw his heart face onto the floor. Clearly, the teacher's control was more important than the toddler's creativity. What terrible thing would have happened if the child had put one or even five extra noses on the face? Would his concept of the human face have been forever warped? Or would he have simply benefited from the fine-motor-development opportunities provided by the pasting on of the heart pieces? Would he have learned something about the shape of the object we call heart and have learned more about faces and features another day? For that toddler, on that day, none of these things occurred because the teacher needed to maintain control. Instead of creating a learning situation, this teacher created a behavior problem.

There is no delicate way to put this. Some adults teach because they like the control that it gives them over children. Having little control in other areas of their lives, they exercise it in the classroom, because children are too little to wrest control back.

If this describes you, you may be creating many behavior problems in your classroom. Difficulties are almost inevitable if the teacher is too controlling, because the young child spends a good measure of his early years fighting for some sort of control over his environment. If he fights against adults who refuse to relinquish even the smallest amount of power to him, then the stage is set for war. Take a look at the list of factors in the "Teacher Control Checklist" provided. Check those items that apply to you. The index will help you know whether you may be too control-oriented. Even if you check only two of the items on the list, consider this: Your need for control may be negatively influencing children's behavior. Perhaps most important, children's opportunities for learning are probably reduced, as are their chances for developing self-esteem.

If this is true of you, don't despair. Try to relax. Try being less concerned about noise and mess, two natural activities of young children. Remember, in allowing the children to be free to behave more naturally you can draw them to you, and in the long run you will gain their cooperation, not lose it.

Strategies for Promoting Positive Behaviors

Once an adult recognizes the extent of her influence on children's behaviors, there are an infinite number of ways to be a positive contributor to this process. Most of these involve introspection and changes in ways of interacting with children and with adults. Other strategies involve a team effort: a revamping of the philosophy and techniques used by an entire staff.

Beginning with the individual teacher, let us examine some suggestions for promoting positive behavior.

1. *Anticipate what is normal for this stage of development.* Review everything you know about children in the age group that you work with. Find out more by reading or talking with others who have expertise. What kinds of developmental changes occur among children

Teacher Control Checklist

Directions: To evaluate the importance of control to you as a teacher or caregiver, read each statement and rate its importance to you and the functioning of your classroom. (If you check more than four items in the "very important" column you may be too control-oriented.)

	Not Important	Somewhat Important	Very Important
1. My classroom must always be clean and neat.			
2. I like the children in my class to be clean and neat.			
3. I have to spend a lot of time giving children directions before an activity.			
4. I must closely supervise every activity in my classroom.			
5. I have trained the children to keep our classroom clean.			
6. Many preschool activities are too messy for me.			
7. Many of the parents of children in my classroom do not discipline their children adequately.			
8. My co-worker is often too lenient with the children.			
9. I find it is often easier to just do things myself rather than have the children do them.			
10. Although the children would like them, there are some activities I refuse to conduct.			

during this phase? What problems are these changes likely to present for the children in your classroom? What fears or frustrations occur as a normal part of development in this phase? By doing so you will be far less surprised by children's behaviors. Don't let yourself be surprised by toddlers' tantrums or by the appearance of aggression in kindergartners.

2. *Reduce opportunities for problem behaviors.* If you know that certain behaviors are normal, minimize situations that can create those behaviors. For example, do not ask young children to sit and be attentive for longer periods than their short attention spans will allow. Do not ask the egocentric toddler to "share" or "wait your turn" for more than a short period. Have extra toys and materials on hand for those children who clamor to play with similar items.

3. *Give children names for feelings and help them learn appropriate ways of demonstrating emotions.* Show them how to show feelings by demonstrating them yourself. Say, "I'm sad today," if it is how you feel. Help a child say, "I'm angry," and if she forgets and hits or cries instead of verbalizing, remember that she is still learning. If a child arrives at school with a specific emotion visible on her face, try saying, "Katrina, are you happy today? Tell me about it. What made you so happy?"

4. *Remember that young children cannot delay gratification of needs in the ways that adults often do.* If a child is cold, tired, hungry, thirsty, or wet, she usually wants that need taken care of immediately. She may cry to indicate the need, or cry in anger or frustration if an adult does not respond quickly enough. Physical and emotional needs (like having an adult remove a fear-producing stimulus) are primary in young children. A teacher who is prepared to meet children's needs under a wide range of circumstances can often avoid problems. For example, bringing an extra snack, a first-aid kit, extra diapers or one change of clothes, and a blanket on a walk can help offset a negative reaction in a young child who has some need that must be quickly addressed.

5. *Avoid overtiring or overstimulating children or placing them in fear-producing circumstances.* One author recalls a colossal mistake she made as a preschool teacher. She had taken her toddlers and their parents on a trip to the local fire station. The toddlers were enthralled by the big engines, the firemen, their big coats and boots. Suddenly the sirens erupted within the station, making a terrific, reverberating noise. Many of the children began to scream in terror. Even after the firemen and engines were gone the children could not be comforted. The morning was a disaster. This possibility should have been considered before the trip.

6. *Do not expect children to move quickly from one activity to another without a transition or adjustment period.* If your first graders are outdoors for recess, they probably spend a great deal of time running about and yelling. When they come indoors that level of energy will be maintained for some time. Children cannot simply turn off their outdoor behavior because someone rang the bell to signal the end of recess. A cool-down activity can help them make the transition to indoor behavior. Music or story time are two examples of successfully used transitional activities.

7. *Permit age-appropriate choices.* This is another aspect of the teacher control issue previously discussed. Choices for children can be wide ranging, from a child's selection of the animal that will be her symbol in the classroom (Laura's is a swan and Elizabeth's is a lion), to the colors and designs chosen by a child for her artwork. Even preschool-aged children can help determine some of their activities during a large-group planning time conducted as part of circle time. Suann Shuster, a wonderful preschool teacher we know, urges her class to submit their suggestions for the daily schedule, regarding the chores that need to be done (like feeding Mr. Lawrence, the class turtle), and the children's preferences for activities and interest centers to be open during free-choice time.

8. *Model good behavior for children.* This means that adults must be willing to observe the same rules that are set for the children. It means that we do not sit on the tables, and that we eat whatever is served at meal times. Suann Shuster has a unique way of modeling potential problems for the children. One day as we observed her in her classroom Suann cautioned the children several times about keeping their feet close to their bodies. They were not very attentive. As we watched, Suann suddenly executed a very convincing pratfall onto the floor. As the children clustered around with concern on their faces, Suann asked, "What happened?" One child quickly volunteered, "Someone had their feet sticking out, and Miss Shuster tripped on them." "What should we do now?" asked Suann. "Keep our feet tucked in," said the children. "Good thinking," said Miss Shuster.

9. *Make your expectations for children's behavior clear.* Young children need a few, clear, simple rules for behavior. Rules like "we do not hit our friends" and "we do not run in our classroom" meet this criterion. Rules should be introduced one at a time, and children should be reminded of them often. We also suggest that rules be written down, even when children are not yet readers. The posting and review of rules on a regular basis can be a powerful reminder of what is expected.

10. *Before children violate rules they should know what the consequences will be.* Telling children that if they continue to throw sand then they cannot play in the sandbox anymore is an example of this. Then, make sure the punishment fits the crime. Teachers have best results with punishments that are swift and related to the misbehavior. Removing a child from a group where she is being disruptive and giving her time out in a quiet area of the classroom can be effective. However, telling a preschooler "When we get back from our walk you will be punished" is often ineffective. After the walk she may not recall the infraction that led to the punishment.

11. *Provide lots of positive reinforcement for children's appropriate behavior.* Even a child's *attempt* at appropriate behavior should be rewarded. You cannot say "nice job" or "good try" or "good work" often enough. Each time praise is given it increases the chances for the appropriate behavior to be repeated. This is where a teacher should put her time and energy, not into reprimands.

Working as a Team to Promote Better Behavior

A good overhaul of the behavior management component of an early childhood program requires that staff members consider the following:

- What am I doing to promote positive behavior?
- What do I do in response to children's inappropriate behavior?
- Do my co-workers have the same philosophy about discipline that I do?
- Do my co-workers and I discipline in consistent ways, or is there a wide variation in our styles?
- Do parents know, support, and agree with our policies?
- If we have an established policy, how old is it? How effective is it? Has the policy ever been evaluated or upgraded?
- What input did individual teachers and parents have in the development of the policy?

As this list of considerations implies, how individual teachers think about and function as part of a team with regard to discipline policies impacts heavily on their success. Time and attention must be given to planning these policies in the same way that time and attention are given to the planning of the curriculum. Adults working in the same setting with young children must be unified in their approach to behavior management. A standard set of techniques must be employed for responding when children are uncooperative or have other behavior problems. When their children enroll in school, parents should be advised about the policies of the program with regard to discipline, including those steps taken by teachers to promote positive behavior.

Ideally, before the first child is enrolled, school discipline policies should be outlined. However, an early childhood staff wishing to develop and implement policies after the fact can easily do so. Here is one process by which policies can be established:

1. Gather all staff members together for a meeting. The topic should be "How We Define Discipline." Brainstorm about what you consider to be desirable behaviors in young children. Consider what the children in your program are really capable of. Write down your expectations as "Goals for Children's Behaviors." For example, "When a child has several toys, he will be able to give one of these toys to another child when that child asks."

2. Have a second meeting and include parents. Discuss appropriate discipline techniques for children in your program. Be certain to hear everyone's point of view, even if you feel that you will be unable to follow their recommendations. Make a list of what appear to be the most effective discipline techniques to come from the session. An example of an appropriate recommendation might be that staff will telephone parents to invite them in for a conference when a child shows evidence of some behavior that is harmful to himself or others, like biting.

3. Have a third, staff only meeting to discuss the outcomes of the previous meetings. Discuss pros and cons, legal issues, and other aspects of your evolving discipline policies. Make a list of final recommendations. These will form the basis of your discipline policies. Remember that the purpose of discipline policies is to state the roles that adults will take in promoting positive behavior in young children.

The final steps in this process are generally up to the program's director or policy board. Someone must make the final decisions and accept ultimate responsibility for implementing the policies. The decision makers should consider the skills and training of the staff, the needs and input of the parents, and the ability of the administrator to effect change, especially if dramatic changes are suggested in existing policies.

Whatever policies are eventually implemented, the discipline policies document should include the reasons or rationale behind the policies, the steps adults can take to encourage children to behave cooperatively, and the specific limits of adult responses to children's misbehavior. For example, an adult should never be permitted to be physically or verbally abusive when disciplining a child. Punishment should never be harsh or prolonged, and children should always have options for improving or changing behavior with the help of adults.

While it is true that every child's situation demands unique and special attention, teachers and caregivers themselves need guidelines to provide a positive, age-appropriate, and stress-free environment for the young children in their care. They need to know how children are affected by the reinforcements that adults provide and how they can alter both the environment and their behavior to give every child the chance to develop into a cooperative and social person capable of giving and receiving affection.

A variety of materials provided at the end of this chapter can help your team effort. The "Sample Discipline Policy" shows you how one center words its policy for staff and parents. "Activities for Teacher Growth" suggests eight different activities for teachers to undertake individually or with co-workers. The "Assessing Classroom Management Skills" tally sheet provides a form for use during observation of a teacher's behavior management techniques.

Acceptable Ways of Disciplining Children

The policies of the Learning Center regarding discipline do not mean that staff wants to permit inappropriate behavior. Instead, the staff wishes to mold or change behavior using positive techniques. To do this, we will:

Develop rules with children that are stated at their developmental level.

Make the consequences for disobeying rules clear before disobedience occurs, for example, "If you hit one of your friends you will not be allowed to play."

Have age-appropriate expectations for children. We do not expect children to understand and obey complex rules.

Allow children time to practice obeying new rules before punishing them. Remember that toddlers have poorly developed memories and may not recall a new rule without lots of practice.

Ignore some kinds of inappropriate behavior. Some misbehavior is an attempt to get attention. The more attention the child gets, the more likely it is that the behavior will be repeated.

Give a time out for other types of inappropriate behavior. A time out is another way of telling a child that his or her behavior is not acceptable. A time out takes a child away from friends and activity for a short time, giving him or her a chance to start over or calm down.

Sample Discipline Policy*

The Learning Center operates on the premise that young children cannot be "bad." The types of inappropriate behavior most often seen in toddler-aged children (including temper tantrums, refusal to cooperate, hitting other children, and failure to follow rules) are usually the result of the child's level of development. A toddler simply lacks the social, emotional, cognitive, and physical skills to comply with many adult demands.

For these reasons the Learning Center staff uses the following guidelines for promoting positive behavior and for responding to problem behavior.

At the Learning Center *we do not hit or paddle children.* Hitting is often misunderstood by a young child, who does not see the connection between a slap and some action on his or her part. Hitting, used as a form of punishment, rarely stops an inappropriate behavior, but does cause confusion and anger.

At the Learning Center *we do not shout or yell at children.* Yelling usually frightens children and distracts them from the problem. Shouting, which is often accompanied by name calling on the part of the adult, also damages a child's self-esteem.

While the Learning Center staff respects the right of every parent to discipline his or her own child in a personal way (except where child abuse or neglect is concerned), parents who volunteer in the Center may not hit or shout at any child. Hitting or shouting at any child, including a parent's own, in the presence of others upsets everyone and disturbs the classroom routine.

© 1992 by The Center for Applied Research in Education

---

*Kathleen Pullan Watkins. *Learning Center Curriculum,* (Philadelphia, PA: Philadelphia Parent-Child Center, 1988), reprinted by permission.

Reinforce desirable behavior by praising the child or rewarding him or her. When the child realizes that attention comes from appropriate behavior, that behavior is more likely to continue.

Role of Parents in the Discipline Process

Children are most likely to respond to attempts to discipline them when the adults involved are consistent, that is, when every adult who disciplines a child uses similar techniques.

Parents often find it difficult to be consistent in times of family or financial pressures or other stresses. They may feel that keeping the child quiet, whatever it takes, is the only solution at that moment.

However, there are other solutions. One of the many roles of Learning Center staff is to work together with parents to help children develop appropriate behaviors. Parents are invited and urged to discuss their concerns about their children's behavior with teachers, and to plan together with staff to respond consistently to problem behaviors. In this way, children will always get the message from the important adults in their lives (parents and teachers) about which behaviors are acceptable and which are not.

Activities for Teacher Growth

Directions: To aid in the evaluation of your own skills for classroom management and guiding children's behavior, complete one or more of the activities below. (They may be conducted by you alone or as part of a group activity in a staff development session.)

1. Make a list of the techniques you use to promote children's positive behaviors.

2. Make a list of all of the discipline techniques you use in response to children's inappropriate behaviors. Divide this list into techniques that are positive and those that may actually reinforce the behavior.

3. Make a list of the ways you collaborate with co-workers to support or help children with inappropriate behaviors.

4. List the techniques you have used for introducing and discussing children's behavior problems with parents. Which of these have been most effective? Why?

5. List the ways in which you have modified the daily schedule/routine to help children make smooth transitions between activities.

6. List all of the types of positive reinforcement you use to reward children for appropriate behavior. Which new techniques can you identify?

7 Discuss with your co-workers your expectations for managing your classroom. Ask for their feedback about the practicality of your "ideal" classroom. Do co-workers feel that your expectations are realistic?

8. Discuss with co-workers the ways children let you know whether or not your classroom management techniques are effective. What modifications can you make in your style?

© 1992 by The Center for Applied Research in Education

Assessing Classroom Management Skills

Directions: This form is for use by a co-worker or supervisor who wishes to give a teacher feedback on his or her classroom management skills. A check or an X may be used to indicate each time that a behavior occurs. After completing the form the observer should consult with the teacher to discuss suggestions for continued growth.

Teacher Name: _____ Observer: _____

Classroom Number/Name: _____

Date/Time of Observation: _____

I. Techniques for Individual Child Management

   A. Supportive Behaviors

      1. Teacher praises child verbally, i.e., "good job!"

      2. Teacher winks or nods at child.

      3. Teacher smiles at child.

      4. Teacher pats or hugs child.

      5. Teacher shares own feelings with child, i.e., "I feel . . ."

      6. Teacher accepts or names child's feelings, i.e., "You must be very angry."

      7. Teacher avoids touching child who does not appear to want to be touched.

      8. Teacher respects child's personal space.

   B. Negative Behaviors

      1. Teacher raises voice to admonish or scold child.

      2. Teacher frowns at child.

      3. Teacher stares at child.

      4. Teacher shakes finger at child.

      5. Teacher speaks sarcastically to child.

      6. Teacher ridicules child.

Assessing Classroom Management Skills (continued)

7. Teacher hugs or touches child who appears to resist touching.

8. Teacher violates child's personal space, causing child to move back or to cower.

II. Techniques for Group Management

  A. Supportive Behaviors

    1. Teacher posts classroom rules.

    2. Teacher discusses consequences for misbehavior with children.

    3. Teacher advises children in advance of the end of activities.

    4. Teacher allows children time to complete projects.

    5. Teacher posts/hangs up all children's artwork.

    6. Teacher uses affectionate terms when talking to group, i.e., "my friends."

    7. Teacher adheres to daily routines and discusses schedule changes in advance.

    8. Teacher makes positive comments about children to parents.

  B. Negative Behaviors

    1. Teacher punishes the group for one or two of children's inappropriate behaviors.

    2. Teacher abruptly makes new rules.

    3. Teacher frequently admonishes children to "stop it" or "be quiet."

    4. Teacher posts/hangs up only "special" or select artwork.

    5. Teacher uses negative terms when referring to children, i.e., "I know you are not all dumb."

    6. Teacher abruptly changes routines.

    7. Teacher breaks promises made to children.

    8. Teacher gives negative feedback to parents about children.

DESIGNING THE ENVIRONMENT TO PROMOTE GOOD BEHAVIOR

Environments influence the people who live and work in them. Children are particularly vulnerable to these influences, as they have fewer strategies for coping or responding to any negative impact from the space around them. In early childhood settings, adults then have a particular responsibility to develop an awareness of the environment's effects. It is important for them to study the ways in which children's development is either enhanced or hindered by the settings in which they spend so much of their formative years. Environments also impact on children's daily behaviors, and the outcome of many a preschool day is determined by the ways in which adults prepare or structure the children's space.

Teachers and caregivers must similarly recognize how their own behaviors and skills may be influenced by their work settings. Environments that are physically and aesthetically pleasing, offer cleanliness and convenience, and are temperature and ventilation controlled are simply more comfortable places to be in. We are more eager to be in them and are more productive when in these spaces than we would be in less suitable spaces.

In this chapter we will explore the tremendous influence that early childhood environments have on children and on the adults who teach and care for them. We will discuss how aspects of the physical and the psychological atmosphere can cause behavior problems. We will also address the impact of environments on other aspects of the children's program, such as the daily schedule and routines set in place in most schools and centers. Finally, we will indicate some mechanisms and tools by which the early childhood environment can be evaluated for its suitability for young children.

Classroom Layout and Children's Behavior

If we were to ask each reader of this book who teaches young children how his or her space came to be arranged, how would he or she respond?

- "I liked it this way."
- "Everything looks nice like this."
- "The parents like things this way."
- "It is arranged to make use of the light and other features of the room."
- "I think this arrangement suits the children."
- "The children helped to arrange the space this way."

It is probably true that most teachers' decisions about classroom arrangement are based on aesthetics—that is, their subjective judgments about an attractive room order. Classrooms are often set up or arranged before the first child sets foot in the room. The adults neither consider the needs of individual children, nor do they seek any direct input from the children about space arrangement. As a result, children come to a strange setting that has been designed for the convenience of the adults who work there. They probably do not feel any sense of ownership of it, which influences their interest in and care of that space. To view this in a slightly different light, consider how many people are careless of others' property while they are fussy and particular in the care of their own things. Children react in similar ways, being less likely to act in destructive ways toward an environment that they feel they own.

Using Interest Centers

An interest center is a defined space in which materials and equipment that fit a specific theme are gathered together for use by one child or several children. Most interest centers are designed for use by small groups of two, three, or four children. Examples of interest centers include library, doll, housekeeping, and block areas. While there are some standard areas that can be seen in many early childhood classrooms, selection of centers should be based on specific criteria, such as the ages and developmental levels of children. Infant centers, for instance, rarely utilize math interest sections but generally include areas for fine- and gross-motor development.

When selecting interest centers, consideration should also be given to the amount of available space. Although offering children six or eight areas to select from might be desirable, doing so might be impossible if space is limited. If this is the case, the number of areas should be limited to those most applicable to children's developmental needs. Failure to consider whether children of a particular age and stage can make use of these areas, or are even interested in them, is a factor in the creation of chaotic environments.

Several considerations determine the placement of interest centers: How accessible are they? What is the relationship of each area to the others? How have traffic patterns evolved? The latter of these must be considered for modification of the space only after teachers have made careful observations.

When considering accessibility, for example, we look at whether the art area has a supply of water nearby or whether one can be made conveniently available. We look at whether children have adequate light for reading or looking at books while in the library area, or whether an additional light source can be provided.

Helping children develop an orderly approach to the use of their space is important, as is teaching them to care for their space. The child using the painting easel is far less likely to drip paint on the floor or to inadvertently smear it on another child if the water and clean-up materials are close to his workspace. A child who can easily and comfortably view a picture book in adequate light will spend a longer time enjoying that book and is less likely to become disruptive or to wander off to another activity.

The relationship of interest centers to each other is a factor in the environment, because the layout either supports or hinders children's play. Consider what might happen if two very busy, dramatic play areas are directly alongside of one another, for example, the housekeeping and block areas. This could, of course, be helpful to children. They might incorporate the blocks and trucks or animal figures (that a good block area has) into house play, or they might build a house of blocks and come into the block area in dress-ups from the housekeeping area to "live" in the block building. Or, there might be some problems as a result of these areas being so close together. If some children, wearing long, loose-fitting dress-ups, wander into the block area from housekeeping, they might accidentally knock over the block structure built by other children. If there are no clear boundaries between these two interest centers children playing with blocks might want to construct some structure on the fringes of the housekeeping area, creating a hazard for children playing there.

Similarly, problems may arise in classrooms where the flow of traffic crosses interest areas where some children are working. Children crossing through a work area may disrupt some children's activities or even cause the destruction of their projects. Watch how traffic patterns evolve in your classroom and modify the layout to minimize disruptions and prevent interference with children's work and play.

The layout of a classroom should also take advantage of a room's natural features. If there are low windows, you will want to keep those spaces open so that children can use them to observe the world outside. If the room has natural nooks or special corner areas, these may be well suited for specific interest centers or perhaps for out-of-the-way storage.

One final recommendation regarding classroom layout is to avoid cluttering children's space and to avoid broad open spaces that invite running. Cluttered areas leave children without sufficient room to spread out and enjoy their play. When they are pushed into small areas they get in one another's way. This can result in quarrels and interference with their creativity. Children are more likely to become disgruntled and to have unproductive play. Wide-open spaces in classrooms also invite inappropriate behavior. Children may take too much unstructured space as a signal to tussle, wrestle, and run.

If we want children to utilize indoor space appropriately we must structure it in ways helpful to them. This includes using all available areas. It also involves placing materials in accessible locations where children can easily obtain them. It is important to remember that materials must be at children's eye level, where they can easily be seen. Young children rarely look up. If displays of materials or photographs are above a child's eye level she simply will not see them. A surprising number of teachers and caregivers even display children's artwork high above their heads. See the "Classroom Layout Checklist" provided to evaluate your classroom layout.

Layout is also important when considering outdoor play spaces. Whether a large or small area is available for play the same set of considerations apply.

- What are the features of the space? Is it level or hilly? Is it wooded or clear? What are its boundaries?
- What is the ground cover? Is it grassy, rocky, sandy, or perhaps cemented over?
- How much, if any, of the space is available for equipment? What is the best arrangement of that equipment?
- Is open space available for other kinds of activities, like riding wheeled vehicles or ball play?
- What are the best uses of the space available? What does the staff hope that children will learn by using this space?

A well-considered layout of outdoor play spaces is essential, because adults have less control over behavior in this space and play tends to be

Classroom Layout Checklist

Directions: To check the suitability of your classroom environment for young children and to assure that the layout of your room does not promote behavior problems, read each item below and check off those that describe your space. For those items you did not check, consider how your layout can be changed.

_____ 1. My classroom has a minimum of four clearly identified interest areas.

_____ 2. Each interest area has discernible boundaries.

_____ 3. All materials designated for children are at their eye level.

_____ 4. All materials designated for children are accessible to them, i.e., not locked in a cabinet or in closed containers.

_____ 5. No windows or doors in my classroom are blocked from view or access by children.

_____ 6. Storage areas or cabinets do not block children's movements or obstruct my view of the room.

_____ 7. Displays designated for children are at their eye level.

_____ 8. Interest centers have sufficient space to accommodate several children at one time.

_____ 9. Placement of my interest centers takes advantage of the natural features of my room (e.g., the library might be near the windows).

_____ 10. Traffic patterns in my classroom do not interfere with children's play.

_____ 11. My classroom has an orderly, uncluttered appearance.

_____ 12. There are no wide-open spaces in my classroom.

less structured. Therefore, the risks to children's health and safety are greater, as are the possibilities for behavior problems. With careful thought and planning, however, outdoor play spaces can be wonderful areas for children's learning and enjoyment.

Like indoor areas, outdoor space can also be modified depending on the group of children and on the skills and concepts being emphasized. While heavy equipment (swings, climbers, sliding boards, etc.) cannot always be relocated, some spaces can be used differently from time to time. For example, you can turn a grassy spot near a fence or wall into a garden during the spring and summer. Using areas for one purpose in the fall months and another during the summer season is another way of making spaces interesting for children. Summer is a good time to bring indoor activities out to the play yard. See the two diagrams provided for some examples of how this can be accomplished.

Creating an Atmosphere for Learning

Each space that people utilize creates a series of physical and emotional impressions. These impressions lead either to our comfort or discomfort while in this area. Classrooms are places where the atmosphere can have a considerable impact on a child's behavior and opportunities for learning.

The atmosphere in a classroom is created by the interactions of two complementary aspects of the environment. One of these is how the space makes us feel physically. This response is created by the lighting, the temperature, the ventilation, even the color of the room. Unfortunately, early childhood staff members do not always have control of these factors.

A second aspect of the atmosphere, however, is very much in the control of teaching staff. It is created by human interactions. The tone set by adults as they interact with children, parents, and with other staff members creates many of the feelings that children have about early childhood settings. The atmosphere of some centers is one of warmth and acceptance. There is a sense that everyone is busy and happy, with little crying and almost no quarreling. In other schools, however, the atmosphere is very different. It is easy to sense people's impatience and tension. The children seem worried and unhappy, and they may show this by crying or arguing with others.

Young children are very sensitive to poor environmental conditions, and especially to an unpleasant atmosphere. In rooms that are too hot or too cold they may become physically or mentally sluggish and unable to participate in activities. They may become tired and cranky because of the discomfort of the environment and become upset more easily by sim-

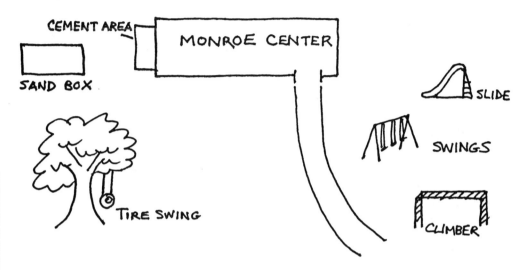

Model 1. The Monroe Child Care Center Play Yard—September

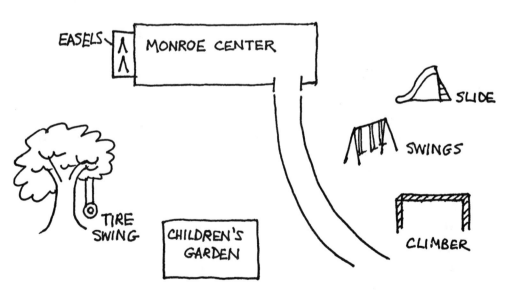

Model 2. The Monroe Child Care Center Play Yard—June

ple problems or events. Compromise with adults or with other children may be much more difficult for them under these conditions.

Similarly, when the human interactions around them are negative, children tend to respond poorly. Even in infancy babies are capable of recognizing and responding to facial expressions, to tones of voice, and to the body language of their adult caretakers. When the atmosphere is stressful children have distinct emotional and behavioral responses that show that they are uncomfortable and unhappy. If adults are conscious of the way these environmental influences affect children, then they can try to control them. While staff members may not be able to make immediate changes in light, heat, or ventilation, they can certainly refer problems to center administrators and recommend changes.

Once they have identified problems, staff members can work together to modify the ways they interact with one another. Sometimes attacking this area involves a rather uncomfortable investigation of adults' feelings and needs to get to the root of group tensions or disagreements that affect the children. One way to begin this process is to use the "Staff Interactions Checklist" that follows as a tool for assessment and discussion.

How Materials and Equipment Can Affect Behavior

Each early childhood education program utilizes materials and equipment to implement its program for children. Materials may be defined as consumables, the paper, paint, crayons, and other items that must be regularly replaced or reordered. Equipment, on the other hand, is of a more permanent nature and includes puzzles, blocks, tricycles, and climbers. Although the presence of all or some of these items is assumed to be a part of most programs, they are rarely thought to have any connection to children's behavior.

Over the years the authors have encountered many instances when decisions about equipment and materials resulted in a number of problems that sooner or later affected the children's behavior and their learning opportunities. Some of these problems include:

- a tendency to order or purchase items based on adult interest in the materials rather than the children's interests.
- a tendency of adults who work with children to covet and collect supplies in their classroom closets rather than to utilize them in the children's program.
- a tendency to leave the same materials on the shelves and in interest

Staff Interactions Checklist

Directions: Use this form to assess the atmosphere created by adult interactions in your program. After completing this checklist individually, be certain to discuss the results with co-workers and to brainstorm about strategies for improving staff relationships.

	Yes	No
1. On arrival in the morning, staff members greet one another pleasantly.	____	____
2. Staff regularly discusses the schedule of activities for children.	____	____
3. Staff shares fully in whatever needs to be done for children during the day.	____	____
4. Staff meets regularly to plan events and activities for children.	____	____
5. Staff has built-in policies or mechanisms for dealing with problems.	____	____
6. Staff avoids gossip about other staff members, parents, or children.	____	____
7. Staff shows loyalty toward the program director.	____	____
8. Staff receives support, as needed, from the director.	____	____
9. Staff regularly receives positive feedback and reinforcement from supervisors.	____	____
10. Staff communicates problems clearly to other workers and supervisors.	____	____
11. In planning absences or vacation time, individual workers take into consideration the needs and schedules of co-workers.	____	____
12. Staff acknowledges the problems or special occasions in the lives of co-workers.	____	____

centers for long periods rather than rotating these with stored materials.

- a failure to organize or categorize supplies so that they may be used in concert with various lessons and themes.
- a failure to regularly inventory supplies so that they can be more efficiently used in concert with planned activities.

These problems with the use of equipment and materials affect children very directly. When supplies purchased meet adult needs rather than those of children, the children often experience boredom or frustration as they attempt to interact with items that are unsuitable for them. Children are also likely to become bored when teachers leave useful supplies on the shelf, while the same books and equipment are available day in and day out. Boredom may also result when teachers are insufficiently prepared to implement themes and activities through the use of classroom supplies. Being hands-on learners, young children must have tactile or other sensory–motor means to experience the concepts or ideas involved. In the absence of these experiences children may fail to grasp the skills being taught and will rapidly lose interest, becoming restless and even irritable.

The selection of classroom and outdoor materials and equipment must be accomplished according to some established criteria (see the "Criteria for Purchase of Material and Equipment," that follows).

Failure to develop or use criteria for selection of materials can create a variety of problems for children.

Equipment that is *not visually interesting* may:
- cause children to be inattentive or disruptive.
- cause children to leave it abruptly without storing it properly.

Equipment that is *insufficiently durable* may:
- lead to accidents and injuries.
- lead to frustration when it fails to hold up under children's exploration.

Equipment that is *not easily stored* may:
- discourage children from participating in cleanup.
- clutter the room and become a cause of accidents and injuries.

Equipment that *has small parts* may:
- lead to frustration when the parts are lost and unavailable during games or other play.
- be accidentally swallowed or otherwise injure children.

Equipment that is *not self-correcting* may:

Criteria for Purchase of Materials and Equipment

Items should

- be age-appropriate.

- be colorful and attractive.

- be durable, and free of breakable parts.

- be useful for teaching more than one skill or concept.

- stimulate the senses.

- store easily.

- relate to other equipment in use.

- fit into an existing or planned interest center.

- be free of small parts.

- be planned for use in a specific lesson or group of lessons.

- build motor skills.

- be self-correcting or require a minimum of adult supervision.

- fit into a sequence of items that facilitate the development of children's skills.

- allow purchase of sufficient numbers for use by several children at a time, or allow use by more than one child simultaneously.

- foster cooperation, not competition.

- extend play rather than limit it.

- promote active, not passive, involvement.

- encourage imagination, not adult control.

- cause children to develop dependent behaviors.
- frustrate children who want or need to know what they have accomplished.

  Equipment in *insufficient amounts* may:
- lead to quarrels among children who are unable to share.
- deprive children of opportunities to contribute to or participate in one another's learning.

Developing Classroom Rules

In this section we will discuss three types of rules found in most early childhood classrooms. These include rules made by adults for children, rules made with children, and rules made by children alone. All three varieties of rules become a feature of the classroom environment. Along with reinforcement that comes from teachers and caregivers, rules are influenced by the environment, which either supports or discourages their acceptance by the children.

Rules Made by Adults

Rules for children serve a wide range of purposes. Whatever the reason for them, an overriding goal is to urge children to conform to some set of expectations. One kind of rule centers around health and safety issues. These are rules that involve areas or activities where children tend to have insufficient information to know how to protect themselves from harm. Although these rules are, in a sense, imposed by adults, children's cooperation with them must actively be sought if the rules are to be observed. Explanations must be provided for inquiring children who need to know "why?" Explanations should be given automatically, even when children do not request them. For example, "Please do not stand on that chair. You could fall off it and hurt yourself."

Rules made by adults and imposed on children should be sensible, and they should be made in relation to children's concrete experiences. It is easier to teach children not to cross the street without an adult (since children encounter streets regularly) then it is to teach them not to talk to strangers. Young children have trouble grasping the concept of stranger.

When rules are introduced to young children they should be introduced one at a time, and adults should provide considerable reinforcement as each new rule is learned. The objects or persons involved in the rule should be pointed out and discussed even when a rule is not being violated. Some examples of this follow:

Example 1

"It is our music time. Would you like to listen to a record? We have to plug in the record player. Do you remember what we learned about plugs and electric outlets? Is it safe for a child to play with a plug? Who is allowed to plug in electrical things? Why do we have a plastic cap on this outlet?"

Example 2

"Tomorrow we go on our trip to the zoo. We will ride on a big bus like we did when we went to the park. Does anyone remember our safety rules? How are we supposed to sit on the seats on the bus? What do we wear when we sit in the seats to help us stay there if the bus stops suddenly?"

Example 3

"It is a very nice day today. I am glad that we came outside for a walk. Here is the street corner where we have to cross. What are our rules for crossing the street safely? What color is the traffic light? Do you see any cars coming?"

Example 4

"It is cleanup time. I see that Courtney and Michael have cleaned up the block area very nicely. What would happen if they left all the blocks on the floor?"

Rules Adults Make with Children

Although some adult-imposed rules are necessary, many early childhood educators have found that those rules that children learn most easily are those that adults make *with* children. These rules may also be related to health and safety but should not involve situations where the children's input could create further hazards for them.

When developing rules with children a teacher sits with the whole group. The teacher poses a situation or problem to the children and asks them to contribute possible solutions. Then the teacher acts as a facilitator to help children arrive at the rule that is in their best interest. A sample situation follows.

A teacher sits with a kindergarten glass at circle time.

Teacher: We need to talk about some problems that children have had while they were playing in the Block Area.

Gayle: Lots of kids have been getting into fights.

Teacher: Why do you think that is happening?

John: Too many children want to play there.

Yvette: There aren't enough blocks for everybody.

Teacher: That is correct. What do you think we can do so that there are not so many arguments?

John: Tell some children to wait.

Teacher: That is a good idea, John. Maybe too many children have been playing in the Block Area at one time. How could we let everyone know how many people are allowed in this area at one time?

Gayle: We could put up a sign.

Teacher: Very good, Gayle! How many children should we have in the Block Area together?

Gayle: Ten!

Yvette: Ten is too many.

Teacher: I think you are right, Yvette. How about five children at one time?

Gayle: Five is good! Will I have to wait a long time to get a turn?

Teacher: No, because we will use the timer that we have in the Housekeeping Area. After ten minutes the timer will ring, and it will be time for other children to take a turn playing with the blocks. Let's go to the Block Area and find a place to put our sign and the timer.

Rules Made by Children

As children in an early childhood classroom begin to become a social group, they also begin to develop and observe rules created by various group members. Some of these rules are stated, and some remain unspoken. Some rules are simple, while others are quite complex. The older the children, the more complicated rules become. Some rules are sensible; others seem nonsensical—at least to adults. These rules may apply when children are gathered in a group with adults present, but most often they apply to children's games and dramatic play. Some rules are derived from those imposed by adults, while others are totally original in nature.

Many early childhood educators are simply unaware of the existence of childrens' rules, and for this reason they remain unaware of how these dictates affect children's behavior. The only way that the rules can be identified is by observing children's play and by asking the children directly. The problem with the latter technique is that children may themselves be unable to state the rules or to recognize them as such. Adults then need to rely primarily on observation to provide clues. Children provide the clues as to the nature of their rules through verbal expression: "No! You can't do that!" Or they may indicate a violated rule through body language or facial expressions that denote the unacceptability of another child's behavior.

Creating rules is an excellent way for young children to develop and exercise social skills. Under most circumstances adults should not intervene to correct or change rules, unless the rules place children in physically or emotionally harmful circumstances. For example, if children are being urged by peers to do something dangerous to earn acceptance, then adults should intervene. If some children ostracize another for reasons of appearance, race, religion, or disability, then a teacher needs to provide information on the meaning of friendship. Awareness of children's own rules can help you understand children's social dilemmas and why certain adult-imposed rules may be frequently violated. It may help you understand how a particular group of children functions as a unit and can also provide the information necessary to help outcast children fit into the group.

Helping Children Observe Rules

One of the goals of competent early childhood professionals is to help children develop self-discipline. Rather than seeing ourselves as disciplinarians, we hope to build into the curriculum and the environment the mechanisms to enable children to grasp the purposes of rules and to gradually be able to abide by them. There are some simple environmental guidelines that can make this process much easier. Let us examine these through the lens of the three elements of the environment: the layout, the atmosphere, and materials and equipment. (One way to quickly assess your current environment is to fill out the "Does Your Environment Support Classroom Rules?" form that follows.)

The *layout* of children's space, as we have already discussed, should be designed with the children in mind. Children's work areas should be clearly their own, while any nonchild areas should also be clearly designated. Rules for children should be posted in a prominent place and means employed to assure that children understand the meanings of the rules. One way to accomplish this is to incorporate pictures, creating easy-to-understand rebuses.

Placing children's materials in areas marked for them helps children know where things belong and where and how to replace them when play is over. It also prevents children from searching for items.

Interest centers can also be labeled to indicate whether they are open or closed during free-choice (free-play) period. A simple "red light means closed, green light means open" system works well in many classrooms. Each area should also be labeled with information to indicate how many children may use it at any given time. Children may not yet be able to

Does Your Environment Support Classroom Rules?

Directions: Use this checklist to determine whether the aspects of your environment (layout, atmosphere, materials and equipment) support the rules for children.

	Yes	No
1. Rules are written down for children.	_____	_____
2. Rules are posted in a prominent place.	_____	_____
3. Rebuses are used for rules designed for non-reading children.	_____	_____
4. Rules are regularly reinforced by adults.	_____	_____
5. Consequences of broken rules are known to children.	_____	_____
6. Adults themselves observe all rules.	_____	_____
7. The physical setting helps children observe rules; for example: • Electrical outlets are covered. • Furniture is child-sized. • Interest centers indicate the number of children that may use an area at any given time.	_____	_____
8. Children's activities are closely supervised by adults.	_____	_____
9. Children are permitted age-appropriate choices.	_____	_____
10. Children are praised for appropriate behavior.	_____	_____
11. Children are forewarned of schedule and activity changes.	_____	_____
12. Adults avoid calling attention to children who misbehave.	_____	_____

recognize and interpret numbers, but they can recognize a series of two, three, or four stick figures that tell them the number of children who may use the sand table or housekeeping area at any given time. Some teachers find that hanging a series of color-coded necklaces near each area is helpful. When a child enters an area she dons a necklace. When he leaves it, the necklace is removed. If a child wishes to play in an interest center and no necklaces are available, she knows that she must wait for her turn to play in that area.

As previously noted, teachers' behavior in the classroom may either encourage rule following or hinder it. We must, first of all, be good role models for the children. Telling them not to sit or stand on tables and then doing it ourselves creates a confusing message. Drawing attention to children who behave inappropriately often has an effect opposite of what we intend. Instead of being embarrassed or thinking twice about disobeying rules, they may take the attention as a kind of reinforcement. Other children who observe this may also decide that misbehavior is a clear-cut way to get into the spotlight.

Reinforcing desirable behavior through praise and reward is a way to encourage children to obey rules. Reinforcements may be given through eye contact, pleasant expressions, touching, or body language. Rewards may be verbal, such as "good job" or "I like the way you _____." A positive response to appropriate behavior might also involve giving children a special treat or a privilege. Each of these types of messages clearly says that the adult is pleased with the child's behavior and hopes it will continue. (Guidelines for using reinforcement will be discussed further in Chapter Six.)

Another way to head off behavior problems is to provide warnings of schedule or activity changes, for example, by announcing, "There are five more minutes to clean-up time." By using warnings, teachers acknowledge the importance of children's work and help them complete one project and prepare for another.

Routines and Schedules

An important aspect of the early childhood environment is the way in which staff members design routines and plan the daily schedule. Children demand consistency from their world and from the adults who manage it for them. When they cannot depend on these things because of frequent modifications, their reactions and behavior tend to become chaotic. We do not mean to imply that occasional novelty is bad for children, only that this should be reserved for special events like holidays or field trips.

For ideal behavior, an appropriate early childhood center's schedule

provides variety.

addresses children's basic needs for food, water, rest, exercise, elimination, and nurturance.

alternates noisy and quiet times.

alternates active and restful activities.

provides for both teacher direction and children's choices.

considers the developmental levels of the children.

provides for language stimulation and enrichment.

offers problem-solving opportunities.

is flexible and open to modification.

accepts a set of changing daily plans developed by teachers.

keeps children occupied.

provides both group and individual time.

Children are not the only ones to benefit from a consistent routine. Adults also need to be able to plan for and anticipate the day's events. Sometimes, however, scheduling is used in negative ways. Adults may assume that the existence of a set of routines is an indicator that no further planning is necessary; if 11:00 A.M. is story time, then any story can be read. In reality, the schedule is only a framework into which teachers plug in their lesson plans and themes for teaching various skills and concepts.

Another negative use of scheduling occurs when schedules are too rigidly adhered to. When children become engrossed in play or in a special project they must occasionally be permitted to see that work to completion. If the schedule for outdoor play or lunch is off by a few minutes there will be no detrimental impact on the children. The results of interrupted work are far more likely to be damaging to children. Asked to stop what they are doing to engage in a significantly less meaningful activity tells children that their work is not important. It certainly promotes feelings of frustration in all children, and some will react destructively with anger.

Used correctly, schedules and routines can be helpful and reassuring to all involved in early childhood programs. Teachers appreciate a schedule that gives them a timetable on which to work and to base the content and length of activities. They can also recognize when and where a slight modification should be made to allow time for some unique activity. It is best though not to disregard the children's routines entirely. Whenever possible, take them to the bathroom and provide meals on time, even while on field trips. The younger the child the more poorly she reacts when basic needs are not addressed. You cannot explain to a recently toilet-trained toddler that there is "no potty here." She cannot and will not wait, and the subsequent toileting accident she will have will affect her behavior for the rest of the day.

While children enjoy and often respond well to special visitors to their classrooms, teachers need to work with prospective visitors to determine whether their presentations will fit into the children's schedule. The benefits of a visit can be entirely lost if the schedule change places too many demands on the children. Here is an example:

> A representative from a local horticultural organization recently visited a Philadelphia day care center. He had planned to show the children how to make terrariums using small plants and two-liter soda bottles. Arriving at 10:00 A.M., he went to work with the children gathered around him at a table, with two teachers assisting. It soon became apparent to observers that the gentleman had not presented to young children before. He directed much of his instruction to the teacher; however, because the teacher lacked sufficient materials to make more than two terrariums, she had little to offer children by way of hands-on experiences. Those children sitting closest to the presenter and teachers were allowed to touch and help with the gardening project, but others did not participate at all. Two hours later, at noon, the children were still seated at the table. They had not gone to the bathroom or risen from their chairs since the activity began. It was one half hour past their scheduled lunch time. All had long since lost interest in the project. Those furthest away from the adults were being admonished to "sit still" or "be quiet" every few minutes.

This was not a learning experience for most of those children. It was wasted time that could have been spent in productive ways. Instead, hungry, tired, and needing to go to the bathroom, the children quarreled their way through lunch preparations, ate sparingly, and did not settle down to nap until it was almost time for midafternoon snack.

It is essential for teachers to be aware of the ways that the environment influences young children. It is also important for teachers to recognize the environment's impact on themselves. In addition to regularly evaluating the environment of their programs to determine exactly how it promotes or hinders children's learning, they must judge whether that environment helps them do their jobs more effectively or prevents them from carrying out job responsibilities. Fortunately for teachers, most of the modifications that will make environments better for children, staff, and even for parents can be made for little or no cost. But, as with other kinds of change, for growth and benefits to be continuous, evaluation must be regular. Asking staff members to annually assess the layout, atmosphere, and materials and equipment in the program is one way to accomplish this end. The rating form included at the end of this chapter ("Evaluate the Center Environment") elicits staff input regarding the environment in areas where administrators may want to consider making changes. The end result of any assessment should be to improve the environment so that children will be able to relax, stress will be minimized along with inappropriate behavior, and children will be helped to reach their full developmental potential.

Evaluate the Center Environment

Directions: Use this form to give input to your center administrator regarding the layout of your classroom or office area, the atmosphere at your center, and the materials and equipment you utilize. Rate each item on this form from one (strongly disagree) to five (strongly agree).

		Strongly Disagree 1	2	Uncertain 3	4	Strongly Agree 5
Layout						
A.	My classroom/work area has sufficient usable space/is uncluttered.	1	2	3	4	5
B.	My classroom/work area has adequate storage.	1	2	3	4	5
C.	I have a secure place to keep my personal belongings.	1	2	3	4	5
D.	There is a place where I can be by myself for a short period.	1	2	3	4	5
E.	My classroom accommodates all the equipment and materials I use to implement the children's program.	1	2	3	4	5
F.	The outdoor play area for children is adequately sized.	1	2	3	4	5
G.	The placement of permanent outdoor equipment (i.e., swings, climber, etc.) is appropriate.	1	2	3	4	5
H.	I enjoy and feel comfortable in my classroom/workspace.	1	2	3	4	5
Atmosphere						
A.	The lighting in my classroom/work area is adequate.	1	2	3	4	5
B.	The temperature in my classroom/work area is comfortable.	1	2	3	4	5
C.	The ventilation in my classroom/work area is sufficient.	1	2	3	4	5
D.	Staff communications in our center are usually positive.	1	2	3	4	5
E.	Staff relationships with parents are generally positive.	1	2	3	4	5
F.	Staff interactions with children are usually positive.	1	2	3	4	5
G.	Expectations of me are made clear.	1	2	3	4	5
H.	I have a schedule of daily events I can count on.	1	2	3	4	5
Materials and Equipment						
A.	I have input into the ordering of work-related supplies.	1	2	3	4	5
B.	My classroom/work area has adequate materials and equipment.	1	2	3	4	5
C.	Materials and equipment for the children are age-appropriate.	1	2	3	4	5
D.	Materials and equipment are not the cause of injuries or accidents in my classroom.	1	2	3	4	5
E.	Materials and equipment are durable and of good quality.	1	2	3	4	5
F.	Children understand the uses of the various kinds of equipment and materials both indoors and outdoors.	1	2	3	4	5

chapter five

IDENTIFYING
BEHAVIORAL PROBLEMS

As the number and kinds of behavioral problems observed in early childhood settings increases, it becomes more difficult to identify the source of a child's difficulties. We do know that all behavioral problems have a cause. At times the cause is organic or physical, but difficulties also arise from social and emotional sources. Poor parenting and family dysfunctions can seriously impair a developing child's ability to successfully interact with others. The purpose of this chapter is to introduce a series of tools you can use to begin assessing behavioral problems. This is the first step in helping children develop the appropriate ways of interacting with others that will enable them to lead rich and productive lives.

How Do You Know It Is a Behavioral Problem?

A behavioral problem in early childhood is not easily definable. This is true because adults have so many different expectations for children under various circumstances and in different settings. Ideally, we would judge children not on adult expectations, but on their unique physical, cognitive, social, and emotional capabilities. For example, should a crying three-year-old accompanying a parent on a 10:00 P.M. trip to a local grocery store be punished because she won't behave? Should we scold a five-year-old who forgets to whisper in the library? Or should the seven-year-old who wants to use her fingers to eat in a restaurant foods that are considered "finger foods" at home be sharply reprimanded about her table manners? All of these examples show how adults apply their standards of behavior and expectations to young children.

We do not mean to imply that we should not help children gradually develop appropriate social behaviors. Rather, we suggest that adults, especially those who work with young children, apply what they know about development to their expectations for children's behavior. This will limit the instances of what we think of as being behaviorally problematic.

So, what definition do we give to "problem behaviors?" Here are some characteristics:

- They interfere with a child's learning, perhaps affecting both the child herself and those around her.
- They pose a threat to the child's health and safety.
- They interfere with the child's social interactions, perhaps making her an undesirable playmate.
- They result in injury to other persons.
- They cause damage to property.
- They are perceived as negative by many other people, both adults and children.

Signals of children's problems do not come only from children themselves. Adults, too, give off indications that a child's problems are serious enough to warrant assessment and identification. Some of these signals include:

- A rise in the caregiver's level of stress.
- Recognition that much of the teacher's attention and energy is being captured by a single child.
- Comments or other hints from co-workers about the caregiver's ability to control a child—perhaps even offers to "relieve" or "take over" for the teacher. (Some co-workers may say, "If that child were in *my* classroom . . .")
- Comments from family and friends about a teacher's change in home or social behaviors. The teacher may be called "edgy" or "nervous" when asked "What is going on at work?"
- A sudden rise in visits to the classroom from a supervisor. This person may appear to be looking critically at the teacher's performance and will probably comment on the child's behavior.
- A series of complaints from parents about the child. She may be involving other children when her behavior is inappropriate, or she may be observed and labeled as problematic based on the parents' own observations.

As we discussed in Chapter Two, many aspects of children's development influence their reactions to people, places, and things. Inappropriate behavior may reflect some developmental delay or health problem, poor nutrition or environment, or other factors.

This chapter contains a number of tools developed expressly to identify behavioral problems. The accompanying text describes the uses (as well as possible abuses) of each form. Our overall emphasis is on identifying problems and their underlying causes so that ultimately the child can receive appropriate assistance. We do *not* mean to imply by the inclusion of so many forms that teachers or agencies should use them all. We merely wish to provide a selection from which forms can be chosen to meet child, family, teacher, and agency needs.

Taking a Child's Health History

Children's health histories remain some of the most useful mechanisms for identifying existing or potential problems at the time of a child's enrollment in an early childhood program, although these records can certainly be referred to at any point that problems are suspected. A carefully constructed health history form (a sample is provided here) examines many aspects of the child's physical and psychosocial development from birth to the present time. It seeks to answer questions about the parent's perception of the child, his skills and abilities, and it helps identify where this perception may play a role in the child's development.

A child's health problems or parents' feelings about a child may actually begin during pregnancy. If parental perceptions of a baby become negative because of a difficult pregnancy, labor, or delivery, it is sometimes difficult to correct the misconceptions. Some children suffer long-term ill effects due to the physical circumstances of their birth. We now know that premature babies, born before they have spent a full nine months in the womb, can suffer developmental delays for many years, even though their recovery appears to be complete. We are not yet fully aware of all of the consequences of parents' addictive behaviors on their children. Mothers and fathers who smoke excessively, drink, or use recreational drugs often have children who have problems lasting throughout childhood.

Over a twenty-five-year period researchers have also studied how an infant's condition at birth influences parents' perceptions of that child. A small, sickly baby may be perceived as vulnerable by his family well into childhood. He may be prohibited from normal explorations or activities because his parents fear he may become ill again or injure himself.

Similarly, a long-term separation of parents and a newborn because of illness may interfere with the normal course of attachment between the parent(s) and child. If prohibited from early interactions and opportu-

Child Health History Form

Child's Name: _____ Age: _____

Address: _____

Telephone: _____

Date of Birth: _____ Sex: _____

Name of Mother: _____

Address: _____

Telephone: _____

Name of Father: _____

Address: _____

Telephone:_____

Parents' Marital Status: _____

Description of Pregnancy: _____

_____

Length of Pregnancy: _____ Child's Weight at Birth: _____

Length at Birth: _____

Type of Delivery (vaginal, Caesarian section, forceps, etc.): _____

_____

Mother's Age at Time of Birth: _____

Father's Age at Time of Birth: _____

Child's Health at Birth (describe any health problems): _____

_____

Was infant hospitalized for any length of time after birth in neonatal intensive care? If so, please describe reasons and length of hospitalization:_____

_____

Child Health History Form (continued)

Number of Mother's Previous Pregnancies: _____

Number of Child's Living Siblings: _____

Age of Siblings: _____

If any other pregnancies were miscarried or stillborn, describe circumstances: _____

_____

Describe child's appearance at birth: _____

Describe child's general behaviors during the neonatal period (first four weeks): _____

_____

Describe feeding method employed by parents in infancy (breast, bottle): _____

_____

Describe child's eating habits in infancy: _____

_____ Now: _____

Describe child's sleeping habits in infancy: _____

_____ Now: _____

Describe child's elimination habits in infancy: _____

_____ Now: _____

Check any family crises or problems that have occurred in child's household:

_____ Separation/divorce of parents   _____ Parent's new job

_____ Death of a family member   _____ Move to a new home

_____ Death of a pet   _____ Birth of a sibling

_____ Serious illness of a family member

_____ Addiction of a family member   _____ Other

Comments: _____

_____

95

Child Health History Form (continued)

Describe child's personality (outgoing/shy; talkative/quiet; energetic/deliberate): _____
_____

Describe child's favorite activities: _____
_____

With what adult does child spend the most time? _____
_____

Does child have opportunities to play with other children? _____
_____

Give child's age in months for first experiences with:

_____ Solid food	_____ Pulling up
_____ Walking	_____ Drinking from cups
_____ Sleeping through the night	_____ Crawling
_____ First words	_____ Using spoon
_____ Rolling over	_____ Standing alone
_____ Climbing stairs	_____ Toilet Training

When did child have first pediatric visit? _____

How frequent are doctor's visits now? _____

Check all of the illnesses that child has had:

_____ Colic	_____ Flu
_____ Scarlet fever	_____ Ear infection
_____ Chicken pox	_____ Rheumatic fever
_____ Diarrhea	_____ Mumps
_____ Headache	_____ Stomach virus
_____ Measles	_____ Cold
_____ Rubella	_____ Other

Child Health History Form (continued)

Insert dates for child's immunizations:

_____

_____

_____

Has child ever been hospitalized (inpatient or outpatient)? Describe circumstances: _____

_____

Has child ever had surgery? Describe circumstances: _____

_____

Does child have any chronic or debilitating illness (diabetes, asthma, etc.)? _____

_____

Does child take any prescription medications? Which ones? _____

_____

Does child take vitamins? _____

When did child have first dental exam? _____

How frequent are visits to dentist? _____

Has child had any problems with nightmares? _____

_____ Bedwetting? _____

Child's usual bedtime? _____

Child's usual waking time? _____

Does child sleep through the night?_____

Does child use a "lovey" at bedtime (special blanket, doll, stuffed animal)? _____

_____

Did or does child use a pacifier or drink a bottle before sleeping? _____

_____

Does parent have any concerns about child's health/development? Please describe: _____

_____

_____

nities to participate in routine caregiving, mothers and fathers may feel that they do not "know" their babies and that their babies do not respond to them. Furthermore, sick newborns often do not look, sound, or respond like full-term, healthy infants. Having a high-pitched cry, being difficult to console, and sleeping for long periods to shut out excessive sensations from the environment can be interpreted by parents as the symptoms of a baby's rejection of them.

Having a successful pregnancy after a number of failed ones may also precipitate problems in the parent–child relationship that ultimately influence the child's behavior. Under these circumstances some parents may react with extreme overprotectiveness, or they may harbor a resentment about the outcome of previous pregnancies that is reflected in their interactions with the child.

An important aspect of the early interactions between parents and their babies involves the parents' degree of success as they attempt to read and interpret infant signals. These are given off by babies as a way of eliciting parents' participation in caretaking routines like feeding, changing, comforting, bathing, and putting the infant to sleep. If the parent cannot meet the baby's needs or the child is perceived as different or difficult, the parent may react by permanently labeling the child. All of the child's behaviors may be interpreted in negative ways.

Children are very directly affected by family experiences, especially those that are traumatic or disrupt family routines. The death of a family member or close friend, even of a family pet, can seriously upset all of the members of a family. Serious physical or mental illness, or problems with addiction can cause untold stress in family members. Parents' changes in career, work locations or schedules, and even a move to a new and unfamiliar home, can easily upset a young child.

Unfortunately, many adults fail to realize the extent to which children are affected by events that influence their families. As a result children may be overlooked in family discussions, learning about events only by eavesdropping on grown-up conversations. Having a limited ability to comprehend adult speech and figures of expression, children create or invent explanations for what is otherwise incomprehensible to them.

With forethought about a child's capacity to comprehend all aspects of a situation, adults can give a child enough honest information about a problem to relieve at least some fears and anxieties. While not all information is suitable for children, a great many elements of most problems can be explained at a young child's level. Adults should remember that even young infants are capable of strong reactions to family problems, not because they are aware of the problems themselves, but because they perceive changes in the emotional state of their caregivers.

When children suddenly become resistant to regular school attendance and begin crying or clinging to adults, parents often suspect that

Tips For Interviewers

When conducting admissions or other interviews of children's parents to obtain information about the child or family, consider the following recommendations for the interview setting and method:

- Schedule interviews for a time and place convenient to the parent(s).

- Select a private place for the interview, where you are least likely to be interrupted by other people or by the telephone.

- Sit side by side with the parent, being careful to avoid putting a desk between you. Make sure the parent is sitting at eye level with you.

- Explain the reason for the interview and the types of questions to be asked beforehand.

- Emphasize the positive outcomes to be gained by sharing information rather than focus solely on any suspect or negative behavior on the part of the child.

- Avoid statements that seem to blame parents or family members for child or family problems.

- Assure the parent(s) of confidentiality.

- If a parent is truly reluctant to share certain information do not apply pressure. Let the parent know that the subject can be discussed at a later time.

- Allow sufficient time for the interview so it can be completed in one sitting. Do not rush parents.

- End the interview on a positive note, suggesting ways that the center staff and parents can work together to help the child. Listen to the parents' suggestions as well.

something is amiss at school. They are often surprised to learn that what the child is reacting to is a problem at home. Aware of the parents' distress, the child becomes reluctant to leave them.

If is helpful for teachers to have information about when children reached various developmental milestones, such as crawling, walking, and speaking first words because significant delays in these areas may indicate health or developmental problems. Illnesses in early childhood, especially preventable childhood diseases, may have left children with developmental problems or disabilities. Furthermore, their very occurrence may signify a pattern of poor health care by the parents.

Just as it is useful to know about the degree and frequency of a child's health care, it is also helpful to know about a child's dental care. Anyone who has ever had a toothache knows how it can influence a person's behavior. A child with sore gums or decaying teeth may be irritable and poorly nourished, since she may be unable to eat.

Knowledge of children's habits is also important. A health history may uncover problems with nightmares or bedwetting. It may also reveal a child's use of a "lovey" (pacifier, doll, stuffed toys) or reliance on a bottle at nap or bedtime.

One word of caution about using any history of a child's health or family. The interviewer should be a sensitive individual, aware of the parent or guardian's perception that the information they are providing is extremely personal and private. The interviewer must be capable of conveying discretion and confidential treatment of privileged information—and of explaining how this knowledge can be used to help a child. If this school or agency representative is successful, a close bond may be established between the staff and the family.

Taking a Family History

Many aspects of ordinary family life can affect children's behavior. Children whose parents have occupations that the child sees as dangerous (i.e., in the armed services, or police or firefighters) may worry a great deal about their parents. They may even feel responsible for the well-being of a parent whose occupation is not dangerous if that parent shows anxiety or stress.

Relationships with siblings and others in the household also influence a child. These relationships may be very beneficial to a child, but if competition is involved or if a household member requires special care that takes attention away from the child, she may become resentful and withdrawn or act out her anger.

The "Family History Form" that follows gives examples of some

Family History Form

Child's Name: _____ Age: _____

Address: _____ Date of Birth: _____

Telephone: _____ Sex: _____

Mother's Name: _____

Address: _____ Telephone: _____

Occupation: _____

Father's Name: _____

Address: _____ Telephone: _____

Occupation: _____

Marital Status of Parents: _____

Activities Child Enjoys with Parents: _____

_____

Siblings of Child

Name	Sex	Age	Name	Sex	Age

Activities Child Enjoys with Siblings: _____

_____

_____

If child does not live with parents, who is primary caregiver? What is relationship to child? _____

_____

List others living in child's household:

Name	Age	Relationship

_____

_____

_____

Family History Form (continued)

Have family members/persons living with child had problems with (check all that apply):

_____ Chronic/terminal illness   _____ Handicapping condition

_____ Depression/mental illness   _____ Child abuse/neglect

_____ Drug/alcohol addiction   _____ Spouse/elder abuse

_____ Marital separation/divorce   _____ Suicide

_____ Teen pregnancy   _____ sudden infant death syndrome (crib death)

_____ Other _____

Comments: _____

_____

_____

Are family problems discussed with child? If so, by whom and how? _____

_____

_____

Are current events discussed with child? If so, by whom and how? _____

_____

_____

Is child permitted to watch television? List types of programs watched and amount of

time child watches: _____

_____

_____

Are child's grandparents living? If so, what is child's relationship with them like? _____

_____

In addition to primary caregivers, what other adults does child spend time with? _____

_____

When parents go out for the evening or go on vacation who takes care of child? _____

_____

types of family problems that have repercussions for many family members. Examples of these include chronic illness, drug dependency, mental illness or severe depression, suicide, and sudden infant death syndrome (crib death). Adults often underestimate the impact these can have on young children.

> A young boy in an early childhood program in Philadelphia began exhibiting psychotic behavior after the murder of his uncle and the crib death of his infant sister. His mother felt that he was too little to understand or be affected by what had happened, and that he was simply causing further problems by "pretending" to be ill. This child was so traumatized by the events in his life that he became emotionally ill. If adults take time to discuss events with children problems can often be averted.

Even when parents or other family members do discuss family problems with a child, knowing how these things are discussed may help teachers and caregivers. Many parents do not really know how to approach children about important and emotional issues. As a result, children become upset or even traumatized by an explanation that only further confuses them.

> When a family pet died, Mrs. R. sought to save her little girl anguish by saying that the cat had "run away to marry another cat." Eventually realizing that the cat would not be back, three-year-old Karen became upset when an announcement came of the impending marriage of a beloved older cousin. It eventually became clear that Karen believed that when her cousin married she would go away and never come back. The young child's preoperational traits that cause her to think only in one way about many events (centration) was the cause of the confusion.

Most of us have heard about the negative influences of television on young children. They are more likely, for example, to exhibit aggressive behaviors after watching a television program containing violence. Even some cartoon shows affect children this way. When children watch programs that show violence or use expensive special effects, an adult needs to be responsible for explaining to the child what is going on. Obviously, it would be better if adults did not allow children to view violent programs, but children *are* watching them. In lieu of the ideal, the practice of allowing children to ask questions and providing honest, age-appropriate answers is one remedy. One of the questions on the "Family History Form" pertains to children's television viewing habits. Knowing how much time a child spends in front of the television set, which programs she watches, and how late they are on can provide many insights into a child's school behaviors.

Some of the questions included in the "Family History Form" may be provocative. They should be asked with delicacy and concern for the parents' feelings. Center staff members should also be prepared to refer families to the appropriate agencies if interviews reveal the presence of serious family problems. Remember that helping a child change school behaviors while doing nothing to influence change in her home environment may very well invalidate all teacher efforts.

Taking a Child's School History

All early experiences affect human development. Some of the effects are positive, while some are not so good. Children of the 1990s are entering some form of schooling at earlier and earlier ages, and even the day care experiences of infants and toddlers influence their development and later school behaviors. The "Child Day Care/School History Form" that follows is designed for use when children have had one or more previous school/day care experiences.

One rather unfortunate feature of these early school experiences is that they are sometimes undertaken because parents have unrealistic expectations for their children's development and school performance. If this occurs, or if the early childhood program is not attuned to the appropriate curriculum and practices for the age group in question, children's first school experiences may be disappointing both for them and for their families. Thus, the types of other programs attended by the child and the frequency of his attendance are significant topics to be discussed with parents. A child's adjustment to school or day care settings may well be affected by how often he attended a previous program.

A child's relationships and reactions to first classmates and teachers, as well as their reactions to him, should also be explored. Any problems in adjustment or behavior experienced in a child's first school situation may be the origin of present problems.

Every child has aspects of past school experiences that he especially liked or disliked. If these can be pinpointed, they may explain some of the child's present behaviors. For example, a parent's comment, "He always hated to play outside because there was a dog in the next yard and he is afraid of dogs" may explain a young child's reluctance to participate in outdoor play.

Parents' own attitudes about the schools or day care centers their children previously attended can also explain the school problems of some children. Even at a very early age children can recognize and respond to negative parental feelings. They can absorb their mother or father's ill will toward or uncertainties about a teacher, and older children recall and will repeat negative remarks made by parents about the school. If parents

Child Day Care/School History Form

Child's Name: _____ Age: _____

Address: _____ Date of Birth: _____

Telephone: _____ Sex: _____

Mother's Name: _____

Address: _____ Telephone: _____

Father's Name: _____

Address: _____ Telephone: _____

Child's Age at Time of First School or Day Care Attendance:_____
_____

First School or Day Care Center Attended: _____

Dates: _____

Types of Program (preschool, playgroup, day care center, Head Start, kindergarten, primary or elementary school): _____
_____

If day care or preschool, describe circumstances of child's attendance (i.e., parents desired peer socialization experience for child, parents' employment): _____
_____

Frequency of Child's Attendance at First Progam (daily/Monday to Friday; twice weekly, etc.): _____

Describe child's reactions to first school experience: _____
_____
_____

Describe child's relationship with first teacher/caregivers: _____
_____
_____

Describe child's relationship with first peer school group: _____
_____
_____

Child Day Care/School History Form (continued)

Other Schools Attended:

Name of School	Type of Program	Dates Attended
_____	_____	_____
_____	_____	_____
_____	_____	_____

Describe any special or unique problems child has had in school: _____

_____

_____

Describe child's school progress as revealed by teacher reports, grades, etc.: _____

_____

How do past teachers/caregivers describe the child? _____

_____

Has child ever cried or acted out when left at school or day care? If so, how did parent react? How did teacher react? _____

_____

What does child enjoy most about school? _____

_____

Does child dislike any aspect of school? _____

_____

Describe parents' degree of satisfaction with child's past school performance: _____

_____

Describe parents' level of involvement in child's school experiences: _____

_____

Describe parents' goals for child's schooling at this time and for the future: _____

_____

_____

_____

feel that the center's staff has failed to show some degree of sensitivity toward them and their child, he will probably do poorly in that program. Parents need to feel that teachers understand and attempt to support their goals for their children. When those goals are inappropriate, staff members must be willing to approach parents with respect and patience to explain why the program functions differently than parents may have anticipated. They may need help to readjust their expectations for their children.

Of course school histories are not relevant for the infant being enrolled in school or for any child starting school for the first time. Also, interviewers should make clear that the reason they are seeking information about previous day care or school experiences is not to assess the performance of other teachers or schools but instead to help identify the causes and solutions of children's difficulties.

Encouraging Parental Involvement

In exploring outside influences on behavior problems, don't neglect parents' previous and current levels of involvement in their children's education. Today we look at parental involvement somewhat differently than in the past. Especially in the day care center, the traditional image of the room mother and of uneasy parents at PTA meetings is inappropriate and out of step with the needs of the working family.

However, when parents are involved in day care and school programs, they maximize their opportunities for direct input into the program in areas such as curriculum, staff hiring, and development. Parental involvement helps parents develop a better grasp of how the program functions. It can help them understand and appreciate teachers' choices of schedules, activities, and materials, and alter inappropriate expectations they may have for their children. When problems arise, these parents have more understanding of how and when the problem occurred and how their children's performance is affected. Close contact with the teaching, administrative, and support staff may also make it easier for parents to receive feedback about their children, especially when those messages highlight a child's problems.

One of the most significant benefits of parental involvement is that it puts parents and teachers together so they may observe and learn from one another. Consider these two examples:

Janet Smith is the loving mother of two-year-old Debby. Janet works, so Debby attends a local day care center. Recently Janet became concerned when she realized that Debby was not making a smooth adjustment to a new classroom. When Debby's caregivers first discussed this with Janet, they assured her that the problem was not serious and could probably be resolved fairly simply. After talking with Janet about possible changes at home to eliminate the possibility of the influence of household stress, the teachers invited Janet to visit the classroom for an hour each morning during the children's arrival time. After watching other parents drop off their children over a period of several days, Janet began to realize that she herself was negatively influencing Debby's adjustment. She realized that she was drawing too much attention to her departure, and may have wanted Debby to cry a little to demonstrate attachment to her. Discussion with the teachers helped support Janet's conclusions that this behavior was not healthy for her daughter, and Janet began to modify her style of departure. Soon Debby's daily tantrums and screams were replaced with smiles and waves as her mother left for work.

Jonathan Jones, a five-year-old kindergartener, was creating problems for both his parents and teachers. He had developed the habit of hitting other children. Jonathan would hit to get a toy he wanted or to get adult attention. He hit when he felt angry with or thwarted by another child. Jonathan's teachers approached this problem very directly. They asked his parents to meet with them, and they talked about possible techniques for responding to his inappropriate behavior. They agreed to adopt a plan, a unified response to each of Jonathan's attempts, successful or otherwise, to hit other children. Jonathan's father also came to school to observe the techniques being used by the teachers. Soon Jonathan's angry outbursts began to abate and his relationships with other children gradually improved.

For parental involvement to be most effective parents must be able to select the form their involvement will take. They need to consider their availability, job and family responsibilities, and special interests and talents. Then, school or center staff can help direct them toward the types of involvement most suitable to them. Of course, under the types of circumstances described in the two examples above, special forms of involvement may be warranted.

Only rarely do early childhood programs seek direct feedback from parents regarding staff performance. Although the reasons for undertaking this kind of evaluation seem obvious, perhaps the most important motive is to assess how effective staff members are in their communications with parents.

When evaluations occur, it is not uncommon for some staff members to become defensive if they feel that their competence is in question. However, the purpose of looking for parental feedback is to examine parents' *perceptions*, as well as what all agree happens in home–school interactions. That is, if parents' impressions are different from those of teachers, then teachers and administrators need to ask why they are different.

Methods of eliciting feedback should also examine the teaching and child-interactive techniques employed in the classroom. Parents cannot understand or support techniques they do not understand, much less adopt them. Evaluating input from parents can be an excellent way of identifying those areas of the program that require further explanation or even a parent-education program. Rather than fearing feedback or taking it personally, staff members should encourage and welcome it.

One final note on this subject. Administrators should take care not to use generalized parental input as a means of gathering information on individual staff members. This negative use of an information-gathering tool can actually harm the parent–teacher relationship. It is not that a teacher's interactions with parents should not be an aspect of evaluating his performance but for parents to honestly convey their feelings about a program, they must be convinced that there will be no negative fallout or repercussions to be dealt with later on.

The two forms that follow are information-gathering tools for parental involvement. The first, "Parental Involvement Questionnaire," can help you bring parents into the center in positive ways; the second, "Parental Feedback Questionnaire," can help you assess parental perceptions of the center and their involvement in it.

Making Effective Observations

Thus far in this chapter we have dealt exclusively with secondary means of gathering information about children, leaving what are perhaps the most important tools for last. These are observation and record keeping. In recent years, we have heard many teachers complain, "Who has time to observe? Who has time for all the paperwork?" Well, it is our contention that no effective teacher can afford not to observe. It should be an activity as natural as talking to children, reading to them, or supervising their play. The early childhood educator must constantly watch his students for signs of stress, developmental delay, and other problems. Direct observation of children yields the most valuable information about childrens' functioning and behaviors.

All children's behaviors should be observed, of course. This is how teachers gather cues regarding their progress, their interests, and their special needs. For the purpose of this book, however, we will focus on problem behaviors and their identification through observation. As already discussed, behaviors merit a special look if they:

- interfere with learning
- pose a threat to a child's health and safety.

Parental Involvement Questionnaire

Child's Name: _____ Age: _____

Parents' Names: _____

Parents' Address: _____

Parents' Telephone: _____

Parents' Occupations: _____

Other Family Members Living at Home:

Name	Age	Relationship to Child
_____	_____	_____
_____	_____	_____
_____	_____	_____

Special Interests or Hobbies of Parents (music, carpentry, sewing, sports, reading, etc.): _____

_____

_____

Type of Involvement Preferred by Parent:

_____ Volunteering at school

_____ Projects at parent's own home

Check those parental involvement activities parent may be available for:

_____ Classroom volunteer   _____ Telephone tree

_____ Field trip chaperone   _____ Collecting/recycling items for class projects

_____ Fund-raising projects   _____ Parent–teacher meetings

_____ Newsletter editing   _____ Pot luck suppers

_____ Center maintenance   _____ Orienting new parents

Parent Feedback Questionnaire

Note to Parents: Our center's staff recognizes the importance of home-school relationships and communications in promoting the development of your children. Please take time to complete this questionnaire to provide us with feedback on our relationship with you. Your opinion and concerns are important to us.

My child's age is: _____ The length of time my child has been in this program is: _____

I have opportunities _____ daily _____ weekly _____ monthly _____ less often than monthly to meet with my child's teacher.

I receive feedback on my child's day or progress from my child's teachers _____ daily _____ weekly _____ monthly _____ less often than monthly.

Feedback on my child's progress is usually delivered to me _____ personally _____ at parent–teacher meetings _____ in writing _____ by telephone.

This feedback is usually _____ a progress report _____ the report of a problem _____ other.

Since enrolling in this program my child has _____ had many problems _____ some problems _____ few problems.

When having to discuss my child with center staff I feel _____ comfortable _____ uncomfortable _____ I have not discussed my child with any staff members.

Parent Feedback Questionnaire (continued)

If my family had a problem that was impacting on my child I

_____ would _____ would not feel comfortable discussing it with a

member of the center staff.

When participating in home-school events, I am _____ made to feel wel-

come _____ not made to feel welcome _____ I have not been involved

in home-school events.

I _____ have _____ have not been invited to volunteer in the classroom.

The teachers'/caregivers' interactions with my child can best be described

as _____ positive _____ satisfactory _____ poor.

The forms of discipline the teachers/caregivers in my child's classroom

use include _____

_____

I _____ am _____ am not satisfied with the discipline techniques used

by my child's teachers.

I receive information about this program _____ daily _____ weekly

_____ monthly _____ less often than monthly.

One aspect of the program that I would like to hear more about is: ____

_____

One aspect of the program that I would like to see changed is: _____

_____

- interfere with social interactions.
- result in personal injury or property damage.
- or, are perceived as negative by others, adults as well as children.

Knowing when to observe is essential for obtaining useful information. At times you know in advance that certain activities are problematic for children. It makes good sense under those circumstances to limit observation times to those that cover those activities. If you are uncertain about what precipitates inappropriate behavior, then several observations scheduled at various times may help you pinpoint problems.

A common misconception is that there is little to observe about children except during free-choice time. Because it is less likely to be teacher directed, this may seem like the ideal time to observe, but observations limited to free-choice time can miss a lot of information. Observations can and should be done at all times of the school day, and every routine and activity should be looked at. Here are a few examples of what we can learn from children during a preschool or day care day.

Circle Time: Teachers can observe a child's ability to attend during an activity; capacity to participate with a group; ability to take turns.

Free-Choice Time: Teachers can observe children's roles as leaders and followers; their skills for dramatic play and role taking; willingness to follow game rules.

Toileting Time: Teachers can observe children's competence with self-care and health skills.

Snack/Meal Times: Teachers can observe a child's ability to socialize during meal times; fine-motor skills; foods liked and disliked; eating habits.

Rest or Naptime: Teachers can observe children's ability to rest and relax at appropriate times; their sleep patterns; whether they are prone to accidents or to disturbed sleep.

Arrival/Departure Times: Teachers can observe children's ability to comfortably separate from parents; children's moods and concerns on arrival at school; the tone of parent-child reunions.

Ideally, of course, you will know what to look for when you observe. In the case of behavior problems the observation time should be spent studying the circumstances around which the behaviors occur. Find the answers to specific questions such as What prompts the behavior? Does there seem to be a cause? What form does the behavior take? How do the children around the child react? How does the inappropriate behavior involve other children? What happens to the child at this time? Does he show specific physical or emotional responses? How does the child react if other children cry or show disapproval? What, if anything, stops the inappropriate behavior? It is essential to develop an accurate picture of all the circumstances that surround problem behaviors (and to understand aspects of health or family histories that may be influential).

Accurate record keeping is the "how" part of the observation equation. Procedures for recording observations of children are slightly different from others in this chapter in that they each generally serve a specific function. For example, if we pick a block of time for observation with the intention of writing down whatever the child says and does during that period, the *anecdotal* style of record keeping is appropriate. (See "Child Observation Anecdotal Record" form provided.) This can help us focus on all of the child's behaviors and interactions during a time span, or it can be used to record a specific event in a child's day, giving an account of what happened under a specific set of circumstances.

Checklists are used to note specific behaviors or skills, such as the presence or absence of a child's social skills. Using a form like the "Checklist for Social Behavior," provided here, a teacher can observe a child during set or specific time periods or over an extended period. As the skills indicated on the list are demonstrated they are either checked off or a date is noted for their appearance. The caregiver may then study the skills or behaviors that have been checked, comparing them with those that are yet to be developed. This information helps create a picture of the way that missing skills may trigger or aggravate behavioral problems.

Yet another record-keeping tool is the *rating scale* like the one provided here. It indicates the frequency with which a child performs some behavior. A teacher could use it to study the ways that a child uses various activity times. Activities in which a child rarely participates or appears uncomfortable can be problem settings, where inappropriate behaviors are more likely to occur.

It is only when the signals of a child's problems are ignored over time that the child becomes difficult to help. While it is painstaking and time-consuming to interview parents and conduct extensive observations of children, the information obtained can provide a strong foundation for helping children develop appropriate behaviors.

Remember that all information, regardless of its source, must be treated with the strictest confidentiality. Parents must be reassured that their business is their own and will be shared only with staff members critical to helping the child. However, it is also true that observations, forms for record keeping, and interviews are not beneficial if left locked in a filing cabinet so that teaching staff have no access to them. Staff members must discuss and share this information and must consult with parents if the outcomes for children are to be positive.

Child Observation Anecdotal Record

Child's Name: _____

Date of Observation: _____ Age: _____

Time of Observation: _____ Date of Birth: _____

Observer: _____

Setting of Observation (place, activity time, etc.): _____

_____

_____

Observation Summary: _____

_____

_____

_____

_____

_____

_____

_____

Findings/Recommendations: _____

_____

_____

_____

_____

_____

_____

_____

Checklist for Social Behavior

Directions: Place a check next to the behavior observed. The absence of a number of social skills may be an indicator of the origin or symptoms of behavioral problems.

Child's Name: _____

Age: _____ Date of Birth: _____

Date of Observation: _____

Time of Observation: _____

Observer: _____

_____ Child joins in group game or play.

_____ Child participates in teacher-led group activity, i.e, circle time.

_____ Child acts as group leader.

_____ Child follows lead of peers.

_____ Child gives suggestions to another child.

_____ Child accepts suggestions of peers.

_____ Child praises peers.

_____ Child accepts peer praise.

_____ Child seeks adult attention in acceptable ways.

_____ Child accepts adult suggestions.

_____ Child seeks adult approval.

_____ Child accepts praise from adult(s).

_____ Child follows adult direction.

_____ Child helps create rules.

_____ Child follows group rules.

_____ Child expresses affection for peers.

_____ Child shows hostility toward adults.

_____ Child shows hostility toward peers.

_____ Child uses adults as source of help/assistance.

Child Observation Rating Scale

Directions: A child's behavior and involvement during various routines and activities may be one way to determine the source of behavioral problems. Use the scale below to rate the child's behavior in these particular activities. Circle the appropriate number.

Child's Name: _____

Date of Observation: _____ Age: _____

Time of Observation: _____ Date of Birth: _____

Observer: _____

	3 = USUALLY	2 = SOMETIMES	1 = RARELY		
1. Child arrives at school in good spirits.			3	2	1
2. Child participates freely in circle activities, i.e., singing, talking.			3	2	1
3. Child engages in dramatic play alone.			3	2	1
4. Child engages in dramatic play with one or more peers.			3	2	1
5. Child participates in table games, i.e., lotto.			3	2	1
6. Child engages in creative or art activities, i.e., music, puppetry.			3	2	1
7. Child builds with blocks.			3	2	1
8. Child selects one or more activities during free-choice time.			3	2	1
9. Child holds and looks at books.			3	2	1
10. Child eats meals and snacks provided.			3	2	1
11. Child rests or naps at appropriate times.			3	2	1
12. Child engages in outdoor play activities.			3	2	1
13. Child participates in clean-up.			3	2	1
14. Child works/plays with members of a group of three or more children.			3	2	1
15. Child works/plays with one-on-one with another child.			3	2	1
16. Child works/plays alone.			3	2	1
17. Child dresses and otherwise prepares self for outdoor play.			3	2	1
18. Child enjoys/participates with visitors to the classroom.			3	2	1
19. Child enjoys/partcipates in walks/field trips.			3	2	1
20. Child welcomes parent(s) at end of day.			3	2	1

chapter six

BEHAVIOR MODIFICATION TECHNIQUES

The terms *behaviorism* and *behavior modification* have always struck a slightly sour note among early childhood educators. The chief reasons for this are that the spokespersons for behaviorist theory (i.e., Pavlov and Skinner) conducted animal research, the results of which they then attempted to apply to human beings. Some also wrote books suggesting ways that the behavior of large groups of people could be changed. Decades ago, one leading proponent of behaviorism even designed a glasswalled, environmentally controlled crib for his child, setting off a storm of national controversy.

To many educators, including those who work with young children, these thoughts and experiments seemed to be something that lovers of human freedom and dignity should despise. The notion of controlling the behavior of others was a frightening threat to all democratic peoples.

Today, however, a closer look at some of the principles of behaviorism reveals ideas applicable in most teaching and parenting situations. In providing a discussion of some of the related techniques, we are not attempting to advocate or endorse behaviorism. We do, however, believe that familiarity with many learning and program models and what each has to offer for classroom practice is essential for teacher survival. No model should be rejected out of hand any more than it should be blindly accepted. In this chapter we will describe what we have found to be useful elements of the behavior modification approach.

What Is Behavior Modification?

It is, simply, a set of techniques developed for changing behavior. It utilizes a system of rewards and punishments to reinforce or to gradually extinguish certain behaviors. Behavior modification has been used in schools for many years, even in preschools. One of the original Head Start models was based on behavior modification techniques. Behavior modification has been widely used in special education to reinforce the learning of disabled children and adults.

Who uses behavior modification? *We all do!* Every gift we give is a form of reinforcement. Think for a moment about why we give gifts. It is true that one reason may be to acknowledge a special occasion. Another reason is to say, "Thank you." But in giving the gift we also say, "Please, go on being who you are to me." We are, in other words, providing reinforcement or encouragement for our relationship to continue. Some greeting cards actually use those words. We hope that every card we send generates a return card from the recipient. If one person stops sending cards (discontinues the reinforcement), the other person may stop as well.

Ordinary manners are a form of reinforcement or reward. Saying "please" or "thank you" is a way of urging family members, friends, and others to cooperate with us now and in the future. Conversely, failure to use manners at the appropriate time causes ill will and lack of cooperation.

At home most parents have a complete system of rewards and punishments that they regularly use to elicit cooperative behavior from their children. Each parent's system is unique or different, usually because the parent has ascertained that the best approach is based on the individual child's needs, likes, and dislikes. Some parents revoke privileges as a way of punishing, while others give special chores or use physical forms of discipline.

Many classrooms operate on a system of rewards and punishments. Teachers who give gold stars, hang up children's work, or let some children run errands are providing a form of positive reinforcement. Teachers who give suspensions, demerits, detention, or use red ink to mark up a student's paper are giving a clear message of disapproval. Of course, not all forms of punishment will be effective. Some children enjoy detention and others do not mind the vacation provided by suspension. Once again, to be effective, the punishments or rewards must be significant to the child.

When modifying behaviors of young children, some of the reinforcements suggested above are not particularly useful. Some of the punishments may even be harmful. The emphasis of our behavior modification techniques will, in fact, be on positive reinforcements. We believe that these are generally the most effective measures for early childhood educators to use, whether to urge children to "keep up the good work" or to change or modify inappropriate behavior. We will stress teachers' uses of verbal comments, facial expressions, touches, and body language as the recommended means to help motivate children to behave appropriately.

Behavior modification becomes a dangerous tool in the hands of an unscrupulous teacher. If it is used to bend or break children's spirits, then it is harmful. If it is used to control children or to rob them of self-esteem, then it becomes a weapon. However, if it is used to guide children to develop skills and behaviors that help them learn, play with others, and achieve success and the approval of society, then behavior modification becomes an effective teaching tool.

The box that follows provides a list of steps to follow in implementing a plan to change a child's behavior. As you will see, the steps are simple and straightforward.

Pinpointing Behavioral Problems

In Chapter Five we discussed mechanisms for assessing children's behaviors. The tools described in that chapter help isolate both the cause and the behavior itself. The authors disagree with those behaviorists who suggest that the causes of inappropriate behavior are irrelevant to the process of changing it. If the misbehavior is the result of some specific event, thing, or person, then removing the stimulus can sometimes stop the behavior. For example, a child who acts out because she is afraid of something will often stop if the person or thing that produces her fear is removed.

Some of the inappropriate behaviors observed in young children cannot be stopped by removing a stimulus, however, since not all causes of misbehavior can be removed. Often, children must learn new ways of responding under these and similar circumstances. They must learn a set of new behaviors that will gradually alter or replace another. Children usually cannot complete this process on their own. They need adults who have a complete picture of the behavior and who have made attempts to understand how the behavior originates or what prompts it. It is essential to have explored this angle of the behavior before developing a plan for modifying it. At times behaviors are simple, but more often they are very complex, influenced by a wide range of factors in the child's personality, family, and environment.

A troubled child may not be terribly selective about when she exhibits inappropriate behavior. She may be disruptive and difficult under a wide range of circumstances. In these situations, to develop a behavior modification plan you may want to focus attention on the behavior alone to help the child begin making changes as soon as possible.

Pinpointing the behavior means naming it very specifically. Saying that a child is hostile for example, is not useful or meaningful, because

Steps in the Behavior Modification Process

1. Specify the behavior to be changed.

2. Identify the circumstances under which the behavior occurs.

3. Specify a goal behavior, the behavior you want the child to exhibit.

4. Determine appropriate reinforcements to be used, based on the surroundings, needs, and interests of the child.

5. Select a reinforcement schedule, i.e., will approximations of behaviors be reinforced? How often will reinforcements occur? How long will the appropriate behavior be reinforced?

6. Implement the program.

7. Evaluate and modify the plan based on its degree of success.

8. Implement the revised plan.

© 1992 by The Center for Applied Research in Education

Common Behavior Problems in Early Childhood

- Hitting
- Sulking
- Biting
- Pinching
- Name Calling
- Whining
- Clinging
- Lying
- Stealing
- Being messy
- Peer rivalry
- Inappropriately demanding attention
- Throwing tantrums

- Saying "no"
- Asking "why?"
- Ignoring adults
- Using inappropriate language
- Refusing to clean up
- Refusing to follow directions
- Destroying property
- Writing on floors, walls
- Teasing
- Telling/tattling on others
- Being bossy
- Refusing to participate

this term does not explain what the child does that is inappropriate. Some examples of pinpointed behavior include:

Instead of . . .	*Pinpointed Behavior*
John is hostile.	John hits other children when angry.
Peggy is disruptive.	Peggy talks loudly at circle and story times.
Thomas is unfriendly.	Thomas has trouble sharing materials with other children.
Joan is disobedient.	Joan refuses to pick up toys at cleanup time.
Terry is immature.	Terry demands attention at inappropriate times.

Pinpointed behaviors tell you precisely what the child does that is a problem for her and those around her. Specifying this behavior is the first step in the process of naming the desired behavior and helping the child attain it. Naming the desired behavior is not always easy. Children may not be capable of the behavior that teachers consider "ideal." Or, it may be difficult to describe the desired behavior because for the child there may be several steps between it and the present inappropriate behavior. Examples of this are provided on the following page.

It is important for adults to accept that children capable of making changes require time and assistance to do so. Even if no transitional behavior is required, the child will still require time to adjust to new expectations, to grasp the reward system, and to practice the changing behavior.

Using Punishment Appropriately

Punishment is the most common technique used by adults for responding to inappropriate behavior. It generally involves some negative response from an authority figure to a child's misbehavior. It may take the form of scolding or reprimanding, removing a privilege, or taking an action against a child, as in spanking. (Since corporal punishment of children is considered inappropriate and ineffective in early childhood settings it will not be addressed as a form of punishment in this book.) In any event, for the child the consequence of punishment is unpleasant.

Punishment has many potentially negative outcomes for children, especially those who are very young. They often fail to make the connection between misbehavior and the consequences enforced by an adult. For example, when four-year-old John began throwing blocks during free-choice time, his teacher removed him from the block area and put him in the time-out chair. John began to kick his feet and cry, saying "Why? Why? I want to play!" John's teacher knelt at his eye level and said,

Inappropriate Behavior	Stage One or Approximated Behavior	Desired Behavior
Child hits other children.	Child tattles on other children.	Child resolves problems with other children by discussion, without physical aggression.
Child will not follow directions.	Child responds to directions when spoken to directly.	Child responds to directions given to group.
Child makes inappropriate demands for attention.	Child waits a short time for attention.	Child waits for his turn.
Child will not clean up after play.	Child cleans up with adult assistance.	Child cleans up own toys after play.

"John, we are not allowed to throw blocks. Someone could get hurt. Do you remember our rule about throwing toys? You must sit in the time-out chair until the timer rings. Then you will be allowed to play again."

For some children, punishment takes an emotional toll, especially if it causes embarrassment or fear. For example, Susan, a six-year-old, was painfully shy. She rarely raised her hand to answer a question in class. She even had toileting accidents because she was afraid to speak out and ask to be excused. Promising to "cure" her of this problem, Susan's kindergarten teacher called on her frequently and made her stand at her desk when she wouldn't answer. Instead of getting accustomed to speaking in front of classmates, however, Susan became even more shy and withdrawn. Now that she is in the first grade Susan's new teacher is taking a different approach. She is encouraging Susan to speak when she is in a small group of only two or three classmates, hoping to work her up to eventually speaking in front of the class.

Punishment causes some children to respond by repeating or continuing a misbehavior. This is most likely to occur when the punishment also inadvertently rewards a child, as when the teacher misjudges what the child likes and dislikes. If the child experiences some positive outcome from the punishment, then the misbehavior is actually reinforced and is more likely to occur again. This happens a great deal more than most teachers realize. Poorly chosen punishment can put a child into contact with another child or toy he wants, can leave him on his own to get into further difficulty, or can draw welcome attention to him.

For example, at story time, three-year-old Lawrence called out loudly to other children, often left the group to run around the room, or teased other children. One of his preschool teachers handled this problem by having Lawrence sit on her lap. The teaching staff met and decided that Lawrence was enjoying the special attention. The staff members resolved that in the future when he misbehaved, Lawrence would be given a time out.

Whenever punishment is used, it must be administered with forethought. It should not be spontaneous. The child should be forewarned about punitive consequences of misbehavior and given opportunities to avoid or stop the misbehavior before any punishment is administered. For example, Ricky usually disrupted circle time in his preschool classroom. The teacher had spoken to him on many occasions about his behavior, attempting to explain that it is hard for other children to participate when Ricky misbehaves. During their last talk, Ricky's teacher told him that the next time he disrupted circle activities he would have to leave the circle. When the behavior recurred, the teacher said, "Ricky, do you remember what I said to you when we talked about how you are supposed to behave during circle time? I am sad that you did not listen to me. You will have to leave the circle. Please go with Mrs. Johnson."

The punishment also needs to be appropriate to the child's developmental level and to the misbehavior. The child should be able to discern the relationship of the punishment to the behavior. For example, Mrs. Jones, a kindergarten teacher, met with the parents of Samantha, one of her students. Samantha's mother described how she handles Samantha's misbehavior at home, telling Mrs. Jones that when Samantha forgets her table manners she is usually sent to her room without her dinner. Mrs. Jones explained that five-year-old children often forget rules and need many opportunities to practice them. She added that Samantha is still growing and every meal is important to her continuing development. Mrs. Jones suggested praising Samantha when she remembers her manners and giving gentle reminders when she forgets.

Especially when children are young, the punishment should not be delayed but should follow the misbehavior. A long delay between the two only confuses a child, who then wonders why the adult is "angry" with her. For example, the staff of the Rainbow Child Care Center often takes children on outdoor walks. Michael had recently had his second birthday and had just started biting other children. During one walk, Michael lifted his partner's hand, and for no apparent reason bit the child's finger. A teacher who witnessed the incident said, "We are not allowed to bite our friends. I'm sorry, Mike. You will have to hold my hand as we walk to the playground, and you will not be allowed to play on the swings today." If this teacher had waited until the group had returned to the center after their walk, the punishment would have lost its effectiveness.

Punishment should never be used by an adult as a way of "getting even" with a child. A child treated in this fashion may himself develop bullying behaviors, since what he is learning is that when one feels thwarted, one should strike back at the offender. It is best instead to respond to the inappropriate behavior impersonally, saying in effect, "I do not like your behavior, but I like you." For example, Mr. Larkin, a first-grade teacher, was asked to meet with the school principal to discuss an incident that occurred during recess. Martina, one of Mr. Larkin's students, was reported to have taken a pen from the teacher's desk. Mr. Larkin dealt with this problem by taking Martina's pen from her until his was returned. The principal explained to the teacher that Martina would not benefit from a retaliatory type of punishment. He suggested that if Mr. Larkin had proof of Martina's stealing, he should talk with her parents and arrive at a punishment that would involve extra work at home or at school.

Here is a review and some pointers on using punishment as a discipline technique.

- Punishment can confuse young children.
- Punishment causes anger and hostility in some children.
- Punishment actually rewards some children.

- Children should be forewarned of impending punishment.
- Punishment should be thought out in advance by adults.
- Punishment should be appropriate to the child's developmental level.
- Punishment should be appropriate to the misbehavior.
- Punishment should be administered soon after the misbehavior occurs.
- Punishment should not frighten or embarrass children.
- Punishment should not be used as a way to "get even" with a child.

Using Rewards and Reinforcement

We eventually want children to recognize the merits of appropriate social behavior; that is, we want them to develop internal or intrinsic motivation to interact with others in positive ways. But before we can help them develop their own reinforcement, we must sometimes provide it for them. Through our knowledge of the growth of individuals and of the development of children in general we are able to arrive at a variety of ways of acknowledging that we are pleased with their behavior.

Behaviorists believe that the use of reinforcement is one of the best ways to build a tendency to repeat appropriate behaviors. Everyday experiences bear out this assumption. When the consequences of our behaviors are positive, we assume that our behaviors are safe and even beneficial to us, so we repeat them.

By adolescence or adulthood we are able to recognize the ways that we may be reinforced by the environment or by our surroundings. We are also significantly less dependent on reinforcement. We can rear children, perform our jobs, and engage in community service without someone constantly saying, "Good job!" Children, however, are not yet so independent of reinforcement. They rely on adult feedback so that they know how and when to change their performance.

We give young children a number of types of reinforcers or rewards to encourage additional appropriate behavior. The type used most frequently is *social reinforcement.* This may be verbal or nonverbal and consists of rewarding children with praise. An adult who smiles at a child, or hugs, pats, or gives her the thumbs up sign is signaling approval. Winks, nods, and even close physical proximity are ways of letting a young child know that your reaction to her behavior is positive. Some of the most effective teachers we have observed convey their opinions to children through a certain kind of eye contact that makes children smile and wiggle with delight. A sheet of "Positive Reinforcement for Young Children's Behaviors" has been provided.

Social reinforcement can also be verbal. Supporting children through the use of expressions like "Nice work!" "Excellent!" or "Good job!" is a very effective way to promote positive behavior. One caution, however, about the use of verbal rewards: They should always be genuine and warm, not forced or artificial. Children can usually discern when adults do not mean what they say.

Appropriate behavior may also be rewarded through permission for *special activities*. Young children enjoy sitting next to a favorite adult at circle or story time, selecting a book to be read or song to be sung, serving the meal or snack to other children, and bringing a special toy to share with other children. Primary school children enjoy a wider range of possible privileges, such as taking a note or book to the office. Awarded privileges should make children feel special without putting them in a position of competition with other children. If a child gains the favor of the teacher but becomes a rival of the other children, then the adult has done nothing to improve the child's circumstances.

Tangible or material reinforcement also has a place in the reinforcement system. When happy faces or other stickers, or badges that say "I'm special!" are given to children, they have concrete evidence of their caregiver's approval. Coloring books and crayons or picture books are small but special ways to reward children. While tangible reinforcement is very useful in a program of behavior modification, and is even useful on a daily basis, teachers should take care not to use it too liberally. Children may become dependent on gifts or presents and may even come to demand material rewards if adults wish them to be compliant. Therefore, the use of tangible reinforcement should be reserved as a special acknowledgment of a child's appropriate behavior.

Positive reinforcement should be used regularly by teachers to urge all children to develop appropriate social skills. It may also be used as one part of a plan to help a child change inappropriate behavior. This is sometimes accomplished through a process called *shaping*, discussed briefly in the section "Pinpointing Behavioral Problems." Shaping refers to a component of a modification plan that calls for a teacher to reward approximations of the desired behavior. At first, the teacher may reward a behavior only slightly different from the one considered inappropriate. Gradually, only behaviors closer to the goal are reinforced, until eventually the approximated behaviors are replaced by acceptable ones.

Jason, a five-year-old kindergartener, had great difficulty during group and circle times. He could not sit still for more than a few minutes at a time. Jason would nudge and push other children and would eventually get up and leave the group to play noisily in another area of the room.

Positive Reinforcement for Young Children's Behaviors

Below are examples of some of the many ways that adults can reward young children for appropriate behavior.

Social Reinforcement (Nonverbal)

- Smiles
- Hugs
- Nods
- Winks

- Pats
- Eye contact
- Shaking hands
- Standing beside

Social Reinforcement (Verbal)

- Good job!
- Nice work!
- Very good!
- Thank you.

- I'm proud of you!
- I like the way that you . . .
- Nice going!
- Excellent!

Activity or Privilege Reinforcement

- Come, sit next to me.

- Will you lead the line?

- You can pick our song today.

- Please bring a toy tomorrow to share.

- Would you like to pick out a story to read?

- Will you help me serve our snack?

- Would like to feed the goldfish?

- Would you like to play in the _____ area?

Tangible Reinforcement

- Stickers
- Stars
- Badges
- Happy faces

- Crayons
- Books
- Coloring books
- Plastic tokens

Jason's teacher developed a behavior modification plan that called for her to gradually shape Jason's behavior until he would be able to fully participate in group times. At first the teacher made it clear to Jason that if he wished not to take part in group activities he had to play quietly in another part of the room. If he was disruptive, he would be put in a time-out chair. Jason did not comply at first and did visit the time-out chair several times. On the third day, however, Jason played quietly and was rewarded with praise from his teacher.

After several days of quiet play Jason's teacher suggested that he stay with the group to sing a song and then he could play alone. He complied with the teacher's request and was rewarded for this small degree of participation with a special sticker to wear on his clothes. Every few days the teacher attempted to prolong Jason's time with the group. When he participated in new ways or stayed longer with his classmates she would reward him. Eventually, Jason was able to fully participate in a group activity, at which point the teacher said quietly, "Jason, we were so glad to have you with us during circle today. Would like you to help me serve the lunch?"

Shaping behavior is useful for adults who work with young children. Many children are not able to make rapid or abrupt changes. Shaping allows them to make gradual adjustments and provides mechanisms to encourage new behaviors.

When attempting to modify children's specific behaviors teachers should not rely indefinitely on the use of positive reinforcement. Gradually, children should incorporate new behaviors into existing ones, and should depend less on reinforcement. Positive reinforcement should, however, be an ongoing part of an early childhood program. Social reinforcement is an important tool that teachers and caregivers have at their disposal for raising the self-esteem of young children and for facilitating psychosocial development. Reinforcement is also a skill used by adults in many social situations. Modeling these techniques for children enables them to grasp the techniques' purpose and to use reinforcement themselves.

Linda is the teacher of two-year-old Marilyn. A typical toddler, Marilyn is not always compliant, and sometimes it becomes necessary for Linda to devise special ways to get her to cooperate. For example, when Marilyn was once reluctant to come to circle, Linda said, "There was once a little girl named Marilyn, who didn't like to come to circle. . . ." Linda went on to tell a tale of a child just like Marilyn who learned how important it was to sing and share with her friends. Linda's story worked and Marilyn came to circle.

Alternative Techniques for Modifying Behavior

Ways of responding to children's misbehavior are not limited to rewards and punishments. A variety of methods can be used to indicate disapproval to children and to promote appropriate behavior.

Behavior Modification Worksheet

Child's Name: _____ Date of Birth: _____

Age: _____

Date of Plan Development: _____

Teacher's Name: _____

Date of Plan Implementation: _____ Date of Plan Conclusion: _____

Behavior to Be Changed: _____

_____

Problems Related to/Associated with the Behavior: _____

_____

Behavioral Goal: _____

Reinforcers Selected: _____

_____

Reinforcement Schedule (specify which behaviors will be reinforced; the circumstances under which they will be reinforced; the frequency of reinforcement; the duration of reinforcement): _____

_____

_____

_____

_____

Timetable for Plan: _____

Modifications Implemented: _____

_____

Outcome of Plan: _____

_____

_____

When children display emotions in negative ways, adults can reflect those feelings back to them by verbalizing them. For example, "Rachel, you seem to be very sad." The adult can further help the child by urging her to explain what is causing her sadness.

Ignoring children's misbehavior is also a useful technique, but it is not always practical. Behavior can be ignored only if it does not threaten the health or safety of the children involved. It cannot be ignored if a child is about to hurt herself severely or is about to hurt another child physically or emotionally. The behaviors that are best ignored include attention-getting devices that children use, such as whining or temper tantrums.

A child may also benefit if an adult provides a variety of outlets for aggressive or angry behavior. Helping children find substitute ways of releasing some emotions can enable them to avoid displays of negative behavior. Sand and water play, creative movement, and artwork (Play doh® and fingerpainting) can help children release upsetting emotions in positive ways.

Sometimes adults must allow children to experience the consequences of their misbehaviors. This is also a form of response that is only appropriate when a child does not risk endangering herself or others. A child may find that unwillingness to share with others can make her an unpopular playmate. When a child treats toys or books roughly she may have to accept that she will not have those toys to play with when she is ready to behave in more constructive ways. As is true of human beings at many phases of their development, children learn best from personal experience despite the efforts of others to share what they have learned.

Removing a child from the scene of misbehavior is a frequently used approach in early childhood classrooms. Placing a child in a time-out chair conveys adult displeasure, but young children do not "think over" their inappropriate behavior as adults often urge them to do. Using a time-out chair or other setting where a child can be temporarily separated from peers should be a way of telling the child that her behavior is unacceptable and that she cannot be a part of the group as long as the behavior continues. Teachers should be cautious about separating a child from the group to make sure that it is not in any way traumatic. Time-out chairs should not face the wall or be placed in a confined space where a child might become fearful.

It is important to mention that the techniques for responding to inappropriate behavior should be as varied and individual as the behaviors themselves. Early childhood educators are as guilty as many parents are of looking for recipes for responding to problems. *There are no solutions that fit every misbehavior.* It is risky, even dangerous, to prescribe responses for behaviors without knowing in detail the child and the circumstances surrounding the behavior. It is difficult, but necessary, for adults to evaluate each child, the misbehavior, and how best to respond to it before they react.

Techniques for Responding to Misbehavior

Some misbehaviors call for a direct and immediate response by adults. The following list describes some ways that teachers and caregivers can react when inappropriate behavior occurs.

- An adult can tell a child how the behavior makes the adult feel, i.e., "When you hit Megan I feel sad."

- An adult can distract a child from inappropriate behavior, i.e., "Matthew, why don't you put down the block and come and see what I found!"

- An adult can remove a child from the scene of the misbehavior.

- An adult can verbalize the child's feelings, i.e., "Courtney, you seem to be very angry. What is making you so angry?"

- An adult can ignore the misbehavior, provided the child is not going to cause harm to herself or to others.

- An adult can put the child into a time-out chair for a limited period.

- If the behavior involves aggression, an adult can provide another means for the child to release it, i.e., through use of water play, a movement activity, puppetry, artwork, or a workbench.

- An adult can allow the child to experience the consequences of the misbehavior, i.e., "I'm sorry that your toy isn't working anymore, Jason, but you threw it on the floor."

© 1992 by The Center for Applied Research in Education

Common Discipline Errors

Most adults react to children's inappropriate behaviors in very predictable ways—angrily and emotionally. They fear the loss of control over a child, and they feel that the child is somehow thwarting them. These strong feelings can cause adults to make mistakes in their efforts to discipline and may actually reinforce the misbehavior. These errors can also stem from the misconception that children's thinking, therefore their ability to comprehend their inappropriate behavior, is very much like that of adults. We often overhear parents and teachers say to children, "Tell _____ you are sorry!" or "Now hug and make up." Demanding that children apologize for their misbehaviors may meet adult needs but is not necessarily helpful to the child, since he may not understand what an apology is. Keep in mind that most children who quarrel over a toy, a game, or adult attention will be playing happily together within several minutes without adult intervention.

Another example of a common discipline error is the use of bribery or threats to elicit appropriate behavior. "You had better put away those toys or you will not be allowed to go outside." "If you eat all of your vegetables tonight, I'll take you to Super Burger tomorrow." These are the common refrains of frustrated adults who feel there is no other way to get children to behave. While the use of threats and bribery may work temporarily, children may become dependent on adult coercion.

Some threats that adults make are meaningless. For example, a teacher may say, "If you don't sit down you won't be allowed to have a snack," knowing full well that she cannot withhold food from a child. The child soon learns that such threats are meaningless and ignores them. They do not influence his behavior in the slightest.

Research on children's development reveals that when adults try to shame or embarrass children what they usually succeed in doing is causing emotional damage. Contrary to some adult opinions, exposing children's misbehaviors to others is not an effective way to stop problems.

Forcing children to compete for rewards or for adult attention can create unhealthy rivalry. Even young children may become jealous if they observe other children receiving the bulk of the positive feedback. Oddly enough, that jealousy can result in further misbehavior, for unrewarded children may strike out at favored children or attempt even more inappropriate means for obtaining attention.

Also potentially problematic are discipline techniques of giving in to whining and tantrums, making comparisons between children, making promises to children that the adult cannot keep, offering choices where none exist, and failing to listen to the child's side of the story.

Common Discipline Mistakes Made by Adults

- Demanding that children apologize.

- Giving in to tantrums or whining.

- Trying to bribe or threaten children to get them to behave.

- Comparing the misbehavior of one child to the appropriate behavior of another.

- Making threats the adults will not carry out.

- Making promises the adult cannot keep.

- Offering choices where none exist.

- Trying to shame or embarrass the child.

- Failing to reward appropriate behavior.

- Rewarding inappropriate behavior.

- Forcing children to compete for rewards.

- Failing to listen to a child's side of the story.

- Making punishments too harsh.

- Forcing a child to share or cooperate.

- Calling a child names.

Measuring Success and Modifying Plans for Behavior Modification

An effective behavior modification plan usually undergoes several revisions. The teacher observes the child to determine the success of several aspects of the plan. How well are reinforcements working? Are reinforcements frequent enough or are they too frequent? Is the child moving toward the goal behavior? Answering these questions tells the teacher whether some revision of the plan may be needed. If a behavior modification plan is not working the reasons may go beyond the child's own reactions to reinforcement. Few early childhood educators work alone in the classroom, with as many as three or four additional adults coming into contact with that child. These professionals or volunteer staff (parents or student workers) must also develop the same set of consistent responses to the child's behaviors. Furthermore, if the child's parents continue to reinforce behaviors that caregivers are trying to change, the behavior modification plan may be doomed to failure. Before the plan is altered in some way, all of the adults involved should be consulted or advised so that they can support the plan's implementation.

Behavior modification can indeed work with young children. Teachers should consider carefully objectives and means for modifying behavior before developing a plan and should guard against motives that involve controlling or breaking a child. If techniques for helping children develop new skills are applied lovingly and with consideration for the children's needs, they can be extremely effective in promoting the children's development.

chapter seven

REFERRING CHILDREN FOR SPECIAL SERVICES

Although there are a great many ways to identify and provide help for children within the school or day care setting, some children's needs are simply outside the realm of the average early childhood educator's expertise. It is often difficult for us to accept that we have done all that we can and must turn to outside specialists for help, but it is sometimes in the best interests of the child. In this chapter we will discuss those situations and the appropriate procedures for referring children to special services.

The process of identifying and contacting outside consultants to help screen, diagnose, and prescribe a program of treatment for a child with special problems is sometimes known as "making a referral." It is crucial that early childhood educators be willing and able to perform this service when something about the child's physical, cognitive, or psychosocial development indicates a serious problem. When we encounter children with behavior problems it is necessary for us to explore all possible reasons for the child's difficulties. Thus far in this book we have examined child rearing, developmental issues, teachers themselves, and the environment as possible causes of behavior. It is not, however, always easy for us to identify the source of a child's problem. Sometimes after looking at the child's history, conducting observations, even changing the environment and attempting behavior modification, it becomes obvious that our efforts to effect change have been unsuccessful. So we look for other input from outside of our school or program to assure that the child's problem is appropriately responded to.

In our society we have many types of specialists available to us. The professions of education, health, sciences, law, and social work, to name a few, provide a variety of specialists dealing with child and family issues. An important part of the growth of the profession of early childhood, and of educators individually, is to develop networks with those individuals who can further enhance our roles and our ability to help children function appropriately and effectively.

When Referrals Are Appropriate

Teachers and caregivers will know that a referral is appropriate only by keeping careful records of what is known about and what has been previously done for a child. Looking at this information and at all attempts to provide help for the child tells us whether the child's needs may outweigh the teachers' and staffs' ability to arrive at some effective solutions.

Referrals may be warranted if a child's school and home functioning are impaired. The child's parents may also provide us with information in this area, as they let us know what their concerns are and about how the child's difficulties affect the family.

Both diagnosed and undiagnosed problems can require outside assistance. Sometimes teachers are completely unable to identify a persistent problem demonstrated by a child that requires assistance. At times, however, teachers may suspect a problem but need outside help in confirming and/or treating it. Two examples follow.

> Michael was a four-year-old student at the Monroe Preschool. While still a toddler, and before starting any school program, Michael had been diagnosed by a private therapist as hyperactive. The staff at the Monroe Preschool knew at the time of Michael's admission that he had been evaluated earlier, but on observation of Michael in the classroom, and following discussions among staff and with Michael's parents, they determined that something else might be wrong. The staff sought permission for Michael's hearing to be tested, and then referred him to a speech and hearing clinic for evaluation. Michael was examined by several specialists, and it was determined that he was not hyperactive but moderately hearing impaired. With amplification through a hearing aid Michael could hear well, and the acting out behavior he had previously demonstrated disappeared.

> Erin was in the first grade. Born prematurely, she had had some speech delay since she first began communicating. Her public school program provided assistance through a speech therapist, but recently some new problems had arisen. Erin's speech progress seemed to be deteriorating. Other children made fun of her, and she was sometimes left out of games and activities or called a "baby." Her teacher decided to call on Erin's father, who admitted that he had also noticed her new behavior. The teacher asked him for permission to have her observed by a consulting psychologist associated with the school district. When the little girl was observed and the psychologist met later with Erin's father, it became apparent that Erin was reacting to some problems going on at home. With some support from the staff and from her family Erin regained her lost speech skills and began interacting normally with other children.

As these examples illustrate, there are times when even though a child has already been evaluated, a second consultation with a specialist may be helpful.

Some behavior problems are directly related to children's special needs. A child's inappropriate behavior may be the direct result of intense frustration over physical limitations such as hearing or visual problems. Even while having a child evaluated for special needs, however, we must help that child understand that some of her behaviors are unacceptable and guide her toward the appropriate behavior. Even severely disabled children must learn techniques for successful social interactions.

As we determine whether a child should be referred for evaluation and special services, we should consider other aspects of the situation in addition to those in the checklist provided. If the child is unable to function successfully with peers, despite adult interventions, this may indicate a more involved problem than center staff can handle. A family history of disabilities or other health problems may mean that the child's behavior requires further investigation by a specialist. As we have previously suggested, the chief issues in determining whether additional help is needed lie in the answers to the questions Have attempts to help this child but been unsuccessful? Do we lack the information, experience, or expertise to help this child reach potential? If the answers to these questions are yes, it is time to seek outside assistance.

Reporting Child Abuse and Neglect

Although it will not be thoroughly explored in this book, some childhood misbehavior can be attributed to child abuse or neglect. Teachers and program administrators should be alert, especially when there is an abrupt change in a child's behavior. A child might begin behaving in an aggressive manner or become withdrawn or suddenly uncooperative. However, a change in behavior alone is not sufficient reason to suspect abuse. Early childhood educators must be familiar with the symptoms of abuse, should consider the signs shown by the child, and should consult with each other prior to taking any action. However, educators are mandated by law to report any suspected abuse causes to the proper authorities, usually the State Division of Children and Youth or Department of Human Services. Policies and procedures for reporting abuse and neglect should be established in every early childhood education program, and they should be reviewed and updated on a regular basis. The telephone number for reporting abuse should be available to each staff member. Staff members should also know that persons making a report in good faith cannot be held legally responsible should the abuse be unfounded, and their confidentiality is usually protected by state law.

When to Refer Children for Special Services

Directions: Use this checklist to help determine whether a child may need to be referred for services outside of the school or day care center. If two or more items are checked consider getting outside assistance with the child's problems.

_____ 1. The child has a problem severe enough to interfere with school functioning.

_____ 2. The problem is undiagnosed.

_____ 3. The child's problem has been diagnosed, but therapeutic efforts to date have not helped.

_____ 4. Plans developed by teachers to help the child have been unsuccessful.

_____ 5. The child's parents have expressed serious concern about the child.

_____ 6. Teachers and staff outside of the child's classroom have taken note of or commented on the problem.

_____ 7. Teachers or other qualified staff have observed the child and agree that outside assistance is needed.

_____ 8. The child's problem interferes with family functioning.

_____ 9. Other children in the classroom are being negatively affected by the child.

_____ 10. The child or family has a family of social, emotional, physical, or cognitive disabilities.

Special Education and the Law

In 1975 a law was passed mandating publicly funded education for children with special needs. It is called the Education Act for All Handicapped Children, or Public Law 94–142. The main provisions of this law are that the exceptional child is entitled to an education that is provided at no cost to the child's family (free), is geared to the child's needs (appropriate), and does not keep the child unnecessarily out of the mainstream (least restrictive).

Children eligible for the special programs that the law provides must first be diagnosed by qualified health personnel as having physical, cognitive, social, or emotional impairment that requires special intervention for them to pursue their education and achieve their full potential.

For children to take full advantage of the programs and services provided, they must attend a publicly funded preschool or elementary school program. However, it may be necessary for a child who is diagnosed as having special needs to transfer into a program that offers the type of services that will benefit the child (at taxpayer expense).

Parents whose children are classified as exceptional are also entitled to special rights. They must be notified in advance, and in their own language, of any meetings in which a plan is being developed for their child. The parents may attend and participate in these meetings, which are usually conducted by a multidisciplinary team. A language translator must be provided for them if needed. If the parents disagree with any aspect of the plan developed, they may request a hearing to have their concerns heard.

Early childhood educators should be familiar with all laws that influence the ways in which they interact with and plan for children and their parents.

Involving Co-workers in Referrals

Teachers should not make decisions on their own to refer children for special services. Other staff members should be consulted before any outside agency or individual is approached. There are many possible roles for co-workers in this process. They may be asked to observe a child themselves and to write a report describing their findings. This is an especially useful role if the staff member does not work with that child on a daily basis. This co-worker provides an experienced, yet possibly more objective, point of view about the child's behavior.

We recommend that all staff members periodically meet to discuss the progress of all children, especially those who may need special assistance. To do this most effectively a format should be developed for presenting each child's case history. This prevents any lapse into inappropriate or unprofessional discussion. A sample format might include:

- A presentation of basic information about the child, such as age, health history, and family history.
- Information on the causes for concern about the child, based on histories, observations, and child behaviors.
- Information on contacts and discussions with the child's parents.
- A discussion of future options and suggestions for assisting the child.

Co-workers may also play a role in meeting and discussing a child's problems with his parents. It is helpful to involve staff members whose relationships with parents are positive and constructive, but not necessarily personal.

Early childhood programs must also determine the degree of involvement that their staff will have during the time that a child is being evaluated by an outside agency. Will they contact the outside agency, or will they require parents to make the contact? At some school and day care centers it is the policy to accompany parents and children to a consulting agency, while at others transportation only is provided. Still others require the parent to make the contact and follow up with an appointment.

A written report of the child's progress to date accompanied by a description of all previous prescriptions or plans to assist the child should be sent to the consulting agency. (See the "Record of Child Referral for Special Needs Evaluation" form that follows.) A copy of this information should be placed in the child's file. Written permission from the parents to refer the child should be obtained if the center staff will be making the contact with the consultants. (See sample form provided.)

It is essential that whatever choices are made about direct involvement of staff during the evaluation period, consulting agencies provide the school with follow-up information regarding the diagnosis and treatment of the child. This information should be provided in writing so that it can be shared with the appropriate teachers and placed in the child's personal file. Of course, if follow-up information is not sent directly to the child's parents, the school should ensure that parents receive it.

Working with Parents

Approaching parents to discuss their children's special problems is never easy, even if the problem is only simple misbehavior. There are many reasons why this is so difficult. Parents themselves sometimes have trouble accepting

Permission to Refer Form

Child's Name: _____ Child's Sex: _____

Address: _____

Age: _____ Date of Birth: _____ Telephone: _____

The _____ has my permission to refer my child,
                 (school)

_____, to _____
       (child's name)   (consulting agency)

for the purpose of _____

_____

I expect to be advised in writing of any outcome of this evaluation.

_____   _____
    (parent/guardian signature)   (date)

Record of Child Referral for Special Needs Evaluation

Child's Name: _____ Date of Referral: _____

Teacher/School: _____

Age of Child: _____ Date of Birth: _____

Referral Consultant/Agency: _____

Description of Child's Special Needs or Problem: _____

_____

Steps Previously Taken to Identify Problems: _____

_____

_____

_____

Consultants or Outside Agencies Previously involved: _____

_____

_____

_____

Outcome of Earlier Consultations: _____

_____

_____

_____

Dates and Discussion Topics of Meeting with Parents: _____

_____

_____

_____

Agency/Consultant to Which Child Is Now Being Referred (include address, telephone):

_____

Purpose of Referral: _____

Desired Outcome: _____

_____

Update on Child's Progress: _____

_____

_____

_____

_____   _____
School Representative   Date

the idea that their children may have problems. They may prefer to feel that the teacher's pinpointing of some negative aspect of their child's development demonstrates the teacher's dislike for the child. They may have misconceptions about developmental problems and their implications. For example, some people believe that a learning disability is a kind of mental retardation. Parents may be convinced that a child's problems are a sign of their own failure to rear a child properly or to provide an appropriate environment.

When parents learn of a teacher's concerns they may react with anger or guilt. They may refuse further assistance or deny that a problem exists at all. Regardless of a family's initial reaction, it is important for teachers and caregivers to gently pursue with parents the need to work together or to secure additional help for the child.

The way a parent is first approached about a child's problems is particularly significant. There should never be a negative or blaming tone taken that implies parental incompetence or increases guilt.

Staff members should consistently reassure parents of their interest in the child and of the existence of positive traits and behaviors. Sometimes it is not advisable to discuss all problems at one time. Parents may respond more positively if information, coupled with some solutions, is provided gradually, over the course of several meetings.

Teachers should alternately listen and talk. That is, a real discussion should go on, with the parents urged to express their own experiences with and reactions to the problem. The keys to success in working with parents are sympathetic listening and constructive and tactful feedback on the possible solutions. (See the "Teacher's Checklist for Meeting the Parents," provided here, as well as the "Parent's Special Needs Checklist.")

If outside consultation is being sought, staff should carefully introduce this idea with reassurances being provided about the confidentiality of personal information and the qualifications of the support service providers. If parents request it, it may be advisable for someone from the school or center to make the initial phone call or appointment for them, or even to accompany the family on the occasion of the first visit to the outside agency. Staff should be careful not to assume parenting responsibilities, but if support at the outset helps increase parents' confidence it may well be worth staff efforts.

Parents should be assured that few problems children have are unresolvable. With early screening, diagnosis, and intervention young children overcome most problems identified in early childhood and go on to have healthy, productive, and happy lives.

Building a Referral Network

Referrals cannot even be attempted if teachers and staff have failed to create a network of outside support services. In preschools, day care centers, and primary schools, such a network is critical. Building a network

Teacher's Checklist for Meeting with Parents

Directions: Use these guidelines to prepare for and meet with parents to discuss a child's problems or special needs.

_____ Plan meetings for a time convenient to both teacher and parents so that neither party feels rushed.

_____ Confirm the meeting the day prior to the scheduled date.

_____ Select a quiet place to meet, where no one will interrupt or over-hear.

_____ Make sure the seating is comfortable.

_____ Assure the parent of confidentiality.

_____ Begin by presenting positive aspects of the child's development.

_____ Discuss the problem honestly.

_____ Avoid blaming parents or the home environment.

_____ Listen to the parent's concerns and issues.

_____ Come prepared with a plan to be discussed.

_____ Seek the parent's input on the plan.

_____ Answer any questions the parent has, or assure the parent that you will obtain needed information.

_____ At the end of the meeting, briefly review the key points.

_____ End on a positive, hopeful note, once again stressing the child's strengths.

_____ Let the parent know what the next steps will be and when their next contact with the agency will occur.

Parent's Special Needs Checklist

Dear Parents:

As we work together to secure help for your child's special needs, we want you to be aware of your parental rights and to be assured that we are operating in your child's best interests. Please read each of the items below and place a check next to those statements that you feel accurately reflect your experience with us. Then consult with the teaching staff so that we can address any issues or questions you may have. Feel free to add any comments.

_____ Teachers approach me in a positive fashion to discuss their concerns about my child.

_____ Teachers and other staff are interested in my point of view and concerns about my child.

_____ I am satisfied that teachers have worked willingly to help my child.

_____ I believe that my child needs additional special help.

_____ Staff members consulted with me before referring my child to an outside agency or consultant.

_____ Staff members have kept information about my child and family confidential.

_____ I have had opportunities to meet or talk with representatives of outside agencies.

_____ I have been invited to participate in meetings held to plan for or discuss my child's progress.*

_____ I have access to my child's records.*

_____ I was informed that I am entitled to a hearing if I disagree with any plans developed for my child.*

---

*These are provisions of federal and some state laws, such as Public Law 94–142.

of support is time-consuming but not difficult. Staff members should begin by familiarizing themselves with community agencies, schools, and businesses. They should know the location of schools into which the graduates of their programs move. They should be familiar with the location and available services of local hospitals and clinics and should get to know, firsthand, neighborhood pediatricians and dentists. Of special interest to early childhood programs should be teaching hospitals with student doctors and nurses, who may be interested in volunteering their services or may be permitted involvement with early childhood programs as a part of their learning experience.

Each community has a set of existing agencies that function to address local needs. (A list of typical agencies has been provided here.) These include associations for mental health, mental retardation and learning disabilities, Big Brother and Big Sister Organizations, facilities for drug and alcohol rehabilitation, and service organizations that help families deal with child abuse and neglect. All of these groups, as well as many others, exist to deal with a community's social problems. These same agencies can be used by day care and school programs to help address the variety of child and family needs that come to our attention. It is making the contacts or connections within various agencies that is time-consuming. Here are some suggestions for getting the networking process underway:

- Send out "letters of introduction" to various community agencies and invite their representatives to visit your school or day care center. (See the sample provided.)
- Schedule an "open house" so that a group of agency representatives can visit and observe your program in action.
- Invite representatives of various agencies to sit on your school's board of directors or your center's policy council.
- Join a local professional group where other agencies are likely to be well represented.
- Schedule children's field trips to sites that fit with curricular themes (such as pediatric or dental offices), so that individuals to whom you might refer children can see them and learn firsthand about the goals of your program.
- Have a fund-raising event, such as a "white elephant" sale or carnival, and ask others to participate or make donations.

Getting to know individuals in various agencies is only a part of the picture. Other questions need to be answered before you can identify the

Community Agencies Providing Special Services

Adoption agencies—assist with home screening, child placement, and follow-up support services.

Alcohol/drug rehabilitation—assist both the addict and family with treatment and recovery issues.

Bereavement counseling—peer groups and therapists work with family members to help them deal with the loss of loved ones.

Big Brother/ Big Sister Organizations—match adult volunteers with children from single-parent families.

Child abuse/neglect hotlines—for reporting suspected cases of child abuse and neglect; this is the legal obligation of teachers/child care workers in most states.

Child guidance clinics—provide programs for the assessment and treatment of a variety of children's psychosocial problems.

Children's aid societies—provide a wide range of therapeutic, supportive, and protective services for children and their families.

Children's hospitals—specialize in the care and treatment of children's health problems; provide outpatient services for the evaluation of developmental delay and disabilities.

Dental schools/clinics—provide preventive and therapeutic treatment of adult and child dental care needs.

Early childhood evaluation centers—specialize in the early screening, diagnosis, and treatment of children's special needs.

Head Start/parent-child centers—provide early childhood education with a strong emphasis on parental involvement for children from eighteen months to five years; some children with disabilities are eligible for services.

Community Agencies Providing Special Services
(continued)

Homeless shelters—provide food, clothing, and temporary shelter for families that have lost their homes.

Homemaker services—provide in-home support for families with primary caregivers that lose their capacity to care for children and perform household responsibilities.

Learning disabilities associations—provide information on learning disabilities and related services, including diagnosis, treatment, and family support.

Legal aid societies—provide free legal services for economically disadvantaged families and individuals.

Mental health/mental retardation associations—provide information on mental health problems and mental retardation and information on available services and special education.

Rehabilitation hospitals—provide therapy and other treatment of diagnosed developmental disabilities and other problems.

Special education resource and information centers—provide a range of parental and support services, materials, and other information on special needs.

Speech/hearing clinics—specialize in the diagnosis and treatment of speech and hearing problems.

State departments of human services—provide a full range of services for the protection and well-being of the child, including the provision of foster care and other protective services.

Sample Letter of Introduction
to Special Service Provider

Monroe Child Development Center
263 West Broad Street
Pleasantown, New Jersey 00000
June 10, 1992

Alyson Martin, Ph.D.
Executive Director
Association for Learning Disabilities
1804 Oak Street
Pleasantown, New Jersey 00000

Dear Dr. Martin:

The Monroe Child Development Center is a nonprofit day care program serving 100 preschool-aged children, from three to five years, and their families.

Our staff has only recently become aware of the fine work that your organization does in the community, and we are interested in sharing information about our agency with you.

We are a child development program in that we support and facilitate the growth of the whole child by providing a safe environment, materials geared to the development levels of the children, and a curriculum geared to their needs and interests. We provide two meals and two snacks daily for children. Our staff has training in child development and early childhood education.

We are interested in creating a network of other organizations and agencies that can provide us with information or services that will further assist our children. We have enclosed a brochure further describing our program and hope that your organization has similar materials that can be shared with us. Should you wish further information please contact us by telephone at 555-5555. We look forward to hearing from you in the near future.

Sincerely,
Yvette Dean
Monroe Center Director

153

NOTICE OF OPEN HOUSE

The Children, Parents, and Staff
of the
Monroe Child Development Center
Cordially Invite Members of the
Education, Human Services, and Business Communities
to an

OPEN HOUSE

Wednesday, October 24, 1990
Ten Until Two O'clock
263 West Broad Street
Pleasantown, New Jersey

Refreshments   Door Prizes   Displays

agencies that can best serve the families and children in your program. For example:

- What is the range of services that each agency provides?
- What are the qualifications of service providers?
- Which age groups are serviced?
- What is the cost of service, if any?
- Is insurance payment accepted? Which types of insurance?
- Is sliding fee scale applicable?
- Is a particular geographic area serviced? If so, what are its boundaries?
- During which days and hours are services available?
- Is public or other transportation available to the service site?
- How long has this agency been serving the community?
- What are the qualifications of service providers?

A questionnaire containing these questions is provided here. Information gathered from it should be organized and cross-referenced according to types of services offered. Putting information on a Rolodex™ for easy access is also helpful.

Parents, teachers, and individuals from the community must work together to pinpoint the child's difficulties and to develop a plan for responding in ways that will help the child eventually achieve full potential. Seeking help from all available resources is one of the professional responsibilities of early childhood educators. It is our profession, working with the very youngest children and their parents, at the outset of the child's school life, that has the opportunity to most positively and effectively influence children's development and functioning.

Questionnaire for Community Agencies/Service Providers

Directions: Our staff is anxious to learn more about your program. Please take time to complete this questionnaire about your services. Thank you.

Agency Name: _____

Address: _____

Telephone: _____

Please describe the range of services provided by your agency: _____

_____

_____

_____

Please describe briefly the qualifications of your service providers: _____

_____

_____

_____

What is the range of costs for your services? _____

_____

_____

What is the age range of the clients that services are provided for? ___

_____

_____

Questionnaire for Community Agencies/Service Providers
(continued)

Are there special criterial for receiving your agency's services? Please check those that apply and discuss below.

_____ Age of client

_____ Clients must have a medical card

_____ Clients must have insurance

_____ Clients must live within certain geographic boundaries

_____ Sliding scale fee payment is applicable

_____ Other (describe): _____

_____

What are your agency's days and hours of operation? _____

_____

Does your agency provide services to clients in their homes? _____

If so, under what circumstances? _____

_____

Is your agency accessible via public transportation? If so, by what routes?

_____

Does your agency provide transportation to your site? If so, under what circumstances?

_____

_____

How long has your agency serviced the community? _____

_____

Are appointments required for visiting your agency? _____

_____

What person(s) may we contact for further information? _____

_____

APPENDIX A

Annotated Bibliography for Parents and Teachers

We have included a large annotated bibliography in this book for several reasons. The first is to provide a series of additional resources for the early childhood educators who use this book. A second reason, however, is to provide resources to which teachers and directors may refer parents. In the process of assisting children with behavioral problems, parents must also be involved. Frequently, a child having problems in school is also having problems at home. His parents may be frustrated and unaware of where they can turn for help. Teachers and program administrators should be familiar with professional resources in the community that can provide counseling or family therapy as needed. In addition, a library of books, or at least a bibliography, that addresses a variety of aspects of child rearing, behavior management techniques, and other aspects of development can be a further source of information. These can be consulted by the early childhood staff members themselves or can be loaned or suggested as reading material for parents.

This list is merely a beginning. We urge you to explore your local library and watch current publications for resource books appropriate for your own library or book list.

Abraham, Willard. *Living with Preschoolers.* Phoenix Arizona: O'Sullivan Woodside, 1976.

Offers a series of short essays on common parenting concerns regarding children in the two- to five-year age range. Interspersed among topics that address schooling/educational issues are essays on discipline and punishment, accidents and safety, fearfulness, independence, and hyperactivity.

Ames, Louise Bates, and Joan Ames Chase. *Don't Push Your Preschooler.* New York: Harper and Row, 1980.

Addresses the reasons parents push young children and the detrimental effects on development and behavior that can result. Describes appropriate parent-child interactions designed to facilitate development.

Bjorkland, Barbara R., and David F. Bjorkland. *The Parent's Book of Discipline.* New York: Ballantine Books, 1990.

The focus here is on discipline in every aspect, including helping a child develop a disciplined lifestyle. Discipline in nontraditional families is explored with a focus on the roles of parents as models for their children.

Bodenhamer, Gregory. *Back in Control: How to Get Your Children to Behave.* New York: Prentice Hall Press, 1983.

Provides a case history approach to dealing with behavior problems. Gives suggestions for discovering the sources of discipline problems and provides techniques for regaining control of disorderly children.

Brenner, Barbara. *Love and Discipline.* New York: Ballantine Books, 1983.

This volume covers a wide range including the role of development in common behavioral problems from infancy through middle childhood. The roles of parental influence on behavior are reviewed, and types of appropriate punishments at various stages are discussed.

Canter, Lee, and Marlene Center. *Assertive Discipline for Parents,* rev. ed. New York: Harper and Row, 1988.

Written by the directors of a national consulting firm that focuses on home and school-related discipline. Helps parents communicate more effectively with children and avoid children's manipulative behaviors.

Cartow, Lonnie. *Raise Your Kids Right.* New York: G. P. Putnam's, 1980.

Provides common sense information on child rearing. Addresses specific discipline techniques while emphasizing the needs of the developing child.

Cherry, Clare. *Please Don't Sit on the Kids: Alternatives to Punitive Punishment.* Belmont, CA: Fearon, 1983.

Describes alternatives to the ordinary adult responses to discipline problems. Formula responses include helping children discuss problems, offering them compliments, praise, and choices, and using humor.

Cherry, Clare. *Think of Something Quiet: A Guide for Achieving Serenity in Early Childhood Classrooms.* Belmont, CA: Fearon, 1981.

Focuses on reducing the stress in children's lives and in their classrooms via rest and relaxation, and communication techniques.

Clark, Lynn. *The Time-Out Solution: A Parent's Guide for Handling Everyday Behavior Problems.* Chicago: Contemporary Books, 1989.

This book includes many specific samples of the origins of problems and ways of coping with them. For example, there is a chart listing the types of rewards children enjoy receiving. There are samples of common child-rearing errors to be avoided, and a discussion of the ways in which adults contribute to discipline problems.

Crary, Elizabeth. *Kids Can Cooperate.* St. Paul, MN: Toys 'n Things Press, 1984.

Teaches techniques for teaching children the skills they need to resolve common conflicts. Contains many exercises.

Crary, Elizabeth. *Without Spanking or Spoiling.* St. Paul, MN: Toys 'n Things Press, 1979.

Provides overview of major child-rearing approaches and advice (for both parents and teachers) on meeting the needs of young children.

Dodson, Fitzhugh. *How to Discipline with Love: From Crib to College.* New York: New American Library, 1977.

This volume focuses on parent-child rapport and its importance in undertaking a mutual problem-solving approach to problems. However, the rights of parents and the proper use of parental "muscle" are also discussed.

Dreikurs, Rudolf, and Pearl Cassel. *Discipline Without Tears: What to do with Children Who Misbehave.* New York: Hawthorn/Dutton, 1989.

Describes a proven approach to classroom discipline for young children via the development of mutual respect. Emphasizes using logical consequences for misbehavior, and focuses on understanding children's motivations for behavior.

Dyer, Wayne. *What Do You Really Want for Your Children?* New York: William Morrow, 1985.

Contains a series of chapters that address what parents want for their children. Each concern is addressed in terms of potential parenting errors and contributions to the child's development.

Elkind, David. *Miseducation: Preschoolers at Risk.* New York: Knopf, 1987.

This book discusses the miseducation of young children in America, that is, the tendency of parents to push their children to develop academic and athletic abilities. Elkind describes the differences between the mind of the preschool-aged child and that of the school-aged child, and describes what an appropriate education for young children is like.

Essa, Eva. *A Practical Guide to Solving Preschool Behavior Problems,* 2d ed. Albany, NY: Delmar Publishers, 1990.

Provides a comprehensive guide to common preschool behavior problems, such as biting and hitting. This volume is divided into seven chapters each covering a different type of inappropriate behavior, such as aggressive/antisocial, disruptive, destructive, and emotional/dependent behaviors.

Faber, Adele, and Elaine Mazlish. *How to Talk So Kids Will Listen and Listen So Kids Will Talk.* New York: Rawson Wade, 1980.

Cartoons, role-playing situations, and exercises are used to help develop communication skills in parents and children. Based on Haim Ginott's theories.

Faber, Adele, and Elaine Mazlish. *Liberated Parents, Liberated Children.* New York: Avon Books, 1974.

While not a new book, this is a useful child-rearing classic designed to help the parent see the child as a person. Discusses the development of autonomy in the child but also focuses on the needs and experiences of parents, including the need to protect children and the inevitable feelings of guilt and anger.

Garber, Stephen W., Marianne Daniels Garber, and Robyn Freedman Spizman. *Good Behavior: Over 1,200 Sensible Solutions to Your Child's Problems from Birth to Age Twelve.* New York: Villard Books, 1987.

Identifies basic discipline problems and techniques for responding to them.

Goldstein, Robin. *Everyday Parenting: The First Five Years.* New York: Penguin Books, 1987.

Addresses the most common child-rearing concerns during early childhood, such as infant crying, separation anxiety and other forms of dependence, the child's use of security objects (blankets, pacifiers, thumb sucking), and so on. Also provides an overview of many facets of early development, including daily routines, the thinking skills of young children, use of toys, and preschool experiences.

Gottesman, David M. *The Powerful Parent: A Child Advocacy Handbook.* Norwalk, CT: Appleton-Century-Crofts, 1982.

Designed as a resource for parents seeking help for a variety of childhood problems. Covers children's physical/medical needs as well as legal, educational, and psychological needs. Provides guidelines for locating professional help and describes the uses of hotlines.

Grisanti, Mary Lee, Dian G. Smith, and Charles Flatter. *A Parent's Guide to Understanding Discipline.* New York: Prentice Hall Press, 1990.

Focuses on teaching love and respect as a mechanism for offsetting discipline problems. Outlines criteria for reasonable expectations for children's behavior and techniques for effective communication. Provides suggestions for dealing with unacceptable behaviors in children.

Ilz, Frances L., Louise Bates Ames, and Sidney M. Baker. *Child Behavior.* New York: Harper and Row, 1981.

Focuses on a broad range of child behaviors and provides advice for parents and professionals for responding to these behaviors. Examples include eating behaviors, dreams, elimination, outlets for tensions, fears, and sexual behaviors. Success in school is the subject of one chapter.

Kelly, Marguerite, and Elia Parsons. *The Mother's Almanac.* Garden City, NY: Doubleday, 1975.

Designed to provide a comprehensive guide to child rearing in the early years. Focuses on the positive aspects of providing support and guidance that will lead to appropriate behavior. Helps adults develop coping skills.

Leatzow, Nancy, Carol Neuhauser, and Liz Wilmes. *Creating Discipline in the Early Childhood Classroom.* Provo, UT: Brigham Young University Press, 1983.

Focuses on problems in early childhood as related to Erikson's stages of psychosocial development. Describes how the classroom can be designed to prevent or offset disruptive behavior, such as through creative use of learning centers. Describes in depth the behaviors that should be modeled by teachers.

Leman, Kevin. *Making Children Mind Without Losing Yours.* New York: Dell Publishing, 1984.

Addresses the role of parental inconsistency in discipline problems. Provides techniques for everyday "reality discipline" and those for becoming your child's "best friend."

Leshan, Eda. *When Your Child Drives You Crazy.* New York: St. Martin's Press, 1985.

Outlines a basic philosophy of parenting. Describes the roles of a child's habits in the parent-child relationship. Discusses aspects of the sibling relationship and the development of sociability in childhood.

Marion, Marian. *Guidance of Young Children,* 2d ed. Columbus, OH: Merrill, 1987.

Provides an overview of the process of guiding children's behavior. Discusses adult influences on children, such as helping children to self-regulate, and provides training to help children resolve their own conflicts. The roles of aggression, prosocial behavior, and self-esteem are discussed.

Mason, Diane, Gayle Jensen, and Carolyn Ryzewicz. *No More Tantrums ... and Other Good News.* Chicago: Contemporary Books, 1987.

Provides a variety of techniques for dealing with preschool-aged children, including techniques for responding to temper tantrums and for responding to some of the causes of tantrums, such as the arrival of a new baby.

Mitchell, Grace. *A Very Practical Guide to Discipline*. Chelsea, MA: Telshare, 1982.

Uses real-life situations to demonstrate effective methods for handling the discipline problems of young children. Focuses on helping children develop self-discipline.

Nelson, Gerald E. *The One-Minute Scolding*. Boulder, CO: Shambhala Publications, 1984.

Billed as an "amazingly effective new approach to child discipline," this volume gives a parent a formula for reprimanding a child. Describes how discipline must be varied depending on the child's stage of development. Also discusses common parenting mistakes.

Snyder, Judy. *I Told You a Million Times . . .* Cary, IL: Family Connections Publications, 1989.

Helps parents of young children examine their styles of parenting and disciplining. Focuses on the importance of mutual respect and self-esteem in the child as methods for encouraging cooperation.

Teaching Good Behavior. Alexandria, VA: Time-Life Books, 1987.

Provides an overview of the ways that misbehavior is manifest in children, such as through negativism, profane language, and bossiness. Suggests mechanisms for teaching children appropriate behavior.

Warschaw, Tessa Albert, and Victoria Secunda. *Winning with Kids*. New York: Bantam Books, 1988.

Includes a focus on negotiation within the family unit. Addresses behavioral issues among children from early childhood through adolescence. Current issues affecting behavior, such as divorce and stepparenting, are addressed.

Williamson, Peter. *Good Kids, Bad Behavior: Helping Children Learn Self-Discipline*. New York: Simon and Schuster, 1990.

A book that focuses on the positive aspects of child rearing, including the use of positive reinforcement and other mechanisms for preventing or offsetting behavioral problems. The role of a child's personality in behavior is discussed, as are suggestions for overcoming the guilt parents often associate with punishing their children.

Yoder, Jean. *The Self-Confident Child.* New York: Avon Books, 1988.

Not a discipline-oriented book per se, this discusses many related issues such as the growth of a child's sense of basic trust and what interferes with it. The stages of the growth of a child's self-esteem are explored, and roles in childhood behaviors.

Ziegler, Norma, Betty Larson, and Jane Byers. *Let the Kids Do It: A Manual for Self-Direction Through Indirect Guidance, Book 1.* Belmont, CA: Fearon, 1983.

The aim of this book is to help adults develop techniques for promoting children's independent behavior. Unique classroom situations are described, along with the use of scheduling, setting limits, establishing routines, and using transitional activities.

Bibliography

Ainsworth, Mary D. Satter, et al. *Patterns of Attachment: A Psychological Study of the Strange Situation.* Hillsdale, NJ: Erbaum, 1978.

Almy, Millie. *Ways of Studying Children.* New York: Columbia University, Teachers College, 1975.

Beaty, Janice J. *Observing Development of the Young Child.* Columbus, OH; Merrill, 1986.

Berger, Kathleen Stassen. *The Developing Person: Through Childhood and Adolescence.* New York: Worth, 1986.

Brazelton, T. Berry. *Working and Caring.* Reading, MA: Addison-Wesley, 1985.

Charlesworth, Rosalind. *Understanding Child Development.* Albany, NY: Delmar, 1983.

Cohen, Dorothy H., and Virginia Stern. *Observing and Recording the Behavior of Young Children,* 3d ed. New York: Teachers College Press, 1983.

David, William E. *Educator's Resource Guide to Special Education: Terms, Laws, Tests, Organizations.* Boston: Allyn and Bacon, 1980.

Gestwicki, Carol. *Home, School, and Community Relations: A Guide to Working with Parents.* Albany, NY: Delmar, 1987.

Greenspan, Stanley, and Nancy Thorndike Greenspan. *First Feelings: Milestones in the Emotional Development of Your Baby and Child.* New York: Viking Penguin, 1985.

Klaus, Marshall H., and John H. Kennell. *Parent–Infant Bonding,* 2d ed. St. Louis, MO: Mosby, 1982.

Lasher, Miriam G., Ilse Mattick, and Frances J. Perkins. *Children with Emotional Disturbance: A Guide for Teachers, Parents and Others Who Work with Emotionally Disturbed Preschoolers.* Washington, DC: Department of Health, Education, and Welfare, 1978.

Marotz, Lynn R., Jeanetia M. Rush, and Marie Z. Cross. *Health, Safety, and Nutrition for the Young Child,* 2d ed. Albany, NY: Delmar, 1989.

Montessori, Maria. *The Discovery of the Child.* New York: Ballantine Books, 1967.

Pulaski, Mary Ann Spencer. *Understanding Piaget: An Introduction to Children's Cognitive Development.* New York: Harper and Row, 1980.

Spodek, Bernard, Olivia N. Saracho, and Michael D. Davis. *Foundations of Early Childhood Education: Teaching Three- Four-, and Five-Year-Old Children.* Englewood Cliffs, NJ: Prentice Hall, 1987.

INDEX